D0475491

TROTH WELLS

SMALL PLANET SMALL PLATES

EARTH-FRIENDLY VEGETARIAN RECIPES

For Milo, and in memory of Copper

Acknowledgements
Thanks to Andy and Ian for the design, and to colleagues at the NI.
Special thanks to William for his support and skills with vegetables, both in growing and cooking them; and to my horsey friends for keeping me going.

First published in the USA in 2013 by

INTERLINK BOOKS
An imprint of Interlink Publishing Group, Inc.
46 Crosby Street, Northampton, Massachusetts 01060
www.interlinkbooks.com

Cover design by Julian Ramirez

Copyright © Troth Wells 2013

Food photography © Kam & Co. Denmark
www.kam.dk

© All other photographs with individual photographers.

All rights reserved. No part of this publication may be reproduced, stored in a retrieval system, or transmitted in any form or by any means, electronic, mechanical, photocopying, recording or otherwise without the prior permission of the publisher.

Library of Congress Cataloging-in-Publication Data available

ISBN 978-1-56656-912-5

Printed and bound in China

To request our complete 48-page full-color catalog, please call us toll free at 1-800-238-LINK, visit our website at www.interlinkbooks.com, or send us an e-mail: info@interlinkbooks.com

MIX
Paper from
responsible sources
FSC® C016973

TROTH WELLS

SMALL PLANET
SMALL PLATES

EARTH-FRIENDLY VEGETARIAN RECIPES

Interlink Books

An imprint of Interlink Publishing Group, Inc.
Northampton, Massachusetts

Contents

Desserts and Drinks

Introduction

IN HIS 1955 PLAY *Visit to a Small Planet*, US writer and political activist Gore Vidal satirized post-war fear of communism, the Cold War and the rising importance of TV. In the play, which was later made into a film, an alien comes to earth to view the American Civil War. The alien miscalculates time and lands 100 years too late, missing the Civil War – but he is delighted to find all the war-toys that have been invented since, and decides to start a war himself.

Some years later, in 1971, Frances Moore Lappé brought a different aspect to the Small Planet idea. Her best-selling book *Diet for a Small Planet* explained how feeding grains to livestock to produce meat for humans was incredibly wasteful both of food and water. She argued forcefully that the only way forward is to eat a 'planet-centered' diet, choosing what is best both for the earth and for our bodies.

It's fascinating to me how both of these works remain so relevant to today's world, and to the concept of this cookbook. Perhaps Islamophobia has taken the place of the Cold War, but war-toys still abound and conflicts are one of many reasons contributing to hunger in the world as people lose their lives and their land in the crossfire. Another key factor is that we do not produce food in a way that is sustainable – in fact we are increasingly going the other way and trying to get more out of each piece of overworked, chemically blitzed land. We are still feeding grain to cattle and other animals that will in turn be fed to humans, instead of using the grain to feed people directly. Worse, we now also grow crops on vast acreage to 'feed' vehicles with biofuels, rather than cutting down on fuel use, in a misguided gesture towards 'saving the planet'.

Our small planet is becoming smaller as resources dwindle, the climate

changes, and the population grows. But we can use what we have in a different, more equitable way, and this can also lighten our impact on the earth. Food is a starting point. No matter how many chemicals are poured onto the land, or industrial farming methods rolled out, or how much farmland is purchased in other people's countries, the current methods of producing food are not going to be enough, even if they were desirable. Ann Gentry, of realfood.com explains: 'Between 2009 and 2010 the world produced enough grain to feed 11 billion people, but humans consumed less than half of it. Where did the rest go? It was distributed as animal feed, and went toward biofuel production. It's easy to see how the less meat we eat, the more grain will be available. Eliminating meat from our diet creates more food for people. Reducing our meat consumption conserves resources and spares the environment.' Of course, there has to be political will to divert plant foods towards people's plates, and that is a major obstacle, but it can be done.

However, non-meat eaters are not only concerned about the waste in the current world food system. Many people choose to be vegetarian or vegan because they don't like the way farm animals are treated, and feel we do not need to kill animals for food – a notion that is entrenched in Buddhism and other religions and philosophies. Even without such guiding frameworks, people turn away from exploiting animals. US writer Alice Walker comments: 'The animals of the world exist for their own reasons. They were not made for humans any more than black people were made for whites or women for men.' A lot has to do with our perspective, as a blogger called Jive noted on HappyCow.net: 'How we see animals is also an important clue in discovering who we are as a species, and what role we fit into within the animal kingdom. Just googling images of the word animal can be a revelation. What you see are pictures of animals at their most proud and majestic. You see cute pics of little baby animals, and animals doing tricks. More important is what

you don't see. What you don't see are pictures of steak.'

I have read blogs and forum posts that wonder what the world would be like without farm animals – would there be significantly less methane from ruminants, for example. Yes. So that would be good for the planet. But it is unlikely that we would have no livestock at all, and I haven't heard anyone argue for that. The issue is that humans do not require meat as part of their diet. All they need can be provided by plant-foods. Even if industrial farming were to end, some people would still keep livestock on an organic, free-range and small scale, and supplies of milk and cheese, possibly some meat, could continue. The point is that the focus would shift from animal-based to plant-based meals, which would be kinder to the animals and to the planet, and better for human health too.

'Increasing consumption of fruits and vegetables and reducing meat intake by half benefits a person's overall health as well as the environment by saving resources and cultivable land,' noted a 2011 study by Vienna University of Technology. The health aspects appeal to some people – one of the most high-profile being former US president Bill Clinton, as reported in the *New York Times*: 'After undergoing two separate heart procedures since leaving office, former President Bill Clinton changed his diet to slow the progression of heart disease. But when a doctor told him that more "intensive changes" were needed for someone with his family history of heart disease, Mr Clinton – the man famous for his love of McDonald's and junk food – went vegan, or nearly so.'

McDonald's will be weeping... but perhaps Bill's damascene conversion will encourage others to have a go at reducing or cutting out meat from their meals. Another prod could be One World Day, on 1 November: 'All you and your friends have to do is agree to eat healthy and sustainable natural, delicious plant-derived foods for at least 24 hours that day.' Or how about Meat Free

Monday (MFM)? Some big name celebs are involved, including Paul, Stella and Mary McCartney. MFM aims 'to raise awareness of the environmental impact of eating meat, and to encourage people to help slow climate change, preserve precious natural resources and benefit their health by having at least one meat-free day every week.' That may be easier for some meat-eaters than going cold turkey – whoops! Paul's first wife, Linda, was a vegetarian and created a wide range of popular veggie foods that have certainly helped shift the vegetarian image from the beans-and-sandals of the 1970s to a more savvy, cool, world cuisine of today.

While the numbers of people calling themselves vegetarian or vegan are not particularly increasing, my own feeling is that people may not choose to label themselves in this way, but actually do not eat meat, or rarely so. One reason for this is that it is so much easier now to find non-meat meals away from home – for example, the HappyCow website furnishes details of veggie cafés and eateries around the world. There is an acceptance that lots of lovely food is plant-based, like the recipes in this cookbook. There is a liberating aspect of non-meat meals, too, in that once you think outside the meat-box, you open up different ways of enjoying food. I particularly like to have a range of dishes on the table, some of which would not 'normally' be there after the 'appetizer/starter' stage. For example, why whisk away the tasty dip when the 'main course' arrives? It could go very nicely with it, or with other vegetable dishes. Some foods which are sweetish, for example corn/maize bread from East Africa or a banana dish from Indonesia, are good accompaniments to savories.

We quite often end up with all sorts of things to have for a meal, often predicated on what is available in the garden or in the fridge and cupboards. Sometimes it can seem rather haphazard, and perhaps this doesn't really go that well with that, but I'm all for trying it. I'm delighted to see that top British chef Hugh Fearnley-Whittingstall is of more or less the same opinion.

11

He writes that his 'tendency now is very much towards meals that give equal weight to several different dishes... There's something particularly enticing about a meal made up of several "small" dishes, such as you get with Middle Eastern mezze or Italian antipasti.' He's right; vegetable cookery lends itself to this pick and mix approach.

So I hope you will enjoy browsing through this cookbook and considering what you might like to try with what. I've put in a few suggestions, but do roam freely and experiment. It's often said that the recipe is just the starting point, and I love it when people say 'I cooked that recipe but I added this and changed that...' Excellent! If enough of us can think differently about food, perhaps we will think differently about how it is produced, and find a way to inspire change on the vast scale needed. But for now, think small – small dishes, lots of them, for our small planet.

Troth Wells

Notes to the recipes

Most of the recipes are vegan or are vegan-adaptable by using soy margarine, milk or yogurt. For green herbs, the quantities in the recipes are for fresh herbs, which give better flavor. But using dried herbs is fine if you cannot get fresh; you would normally use a smaller amount – 1 tablespoon of fresh parsley would be about 1 teaspoon of dried.

V = vegan

Va = vegan-adaptable

I saw a man,

An old Cilician, who occupied

An acre or two of land that no-one wanted,

A patch not worth the ploughing, unrewarding

For flocks, unfit for vineyards; he however

By planting here and there among the scrub

Cabbages and white lilies and verbena

And flimsy poppies, fancied himself a king

In wealth, and coming home late in the evening

Loaded his board with unbought delicacies.

— Virgil, *The Georgics* (29 BCE)

Dishes on following spread: Mashed spicy eggplant/aubergine; Bean and pumpkin stew; Fragrant avocado dip; Marinated cabbage salad; Coconut rice.

Versatile avos – great on toast, in dips, in milkshakes and ice cream. They are high in monounsaturated fats, potassium, B vitamins and fiber. It's lucky they also taste so good! Here's a lovely, easy **Mexican**-style meal. You can fill the tacos with a variety of mixtures, including the Ethiopian peanut stew (p82) and also *frijoles* from the fajita recipe (p36).

SERVES
2-4

TAKES
10 minutes

Avocado tacos

V_a

8 taco shells

For the filling:
2 avocados
2 cloves garlic, crushed
¼-½ teaspoon chili powder
2 teaspoons lime or lemon juice
1 tomato, chopped
1 cup / 110 g cheddar cheese, grated +
salt

+ optional

1 To make the filling, scoop out the avocado pulp into a bowl and combine with the garlic, chili powder and lime or lemon juice, and salt as required.

2 Now heat the tacos according to the packet instructions.

3 Fill the warmed tacos and serve with the chopped tomato and cheese. Eat at once, with salad on the side.

You can also use:

Fajitas mix p36
Groundnut/Peanut stew mix p82

Even though beancurd/tofu is thought to have been created by a Chinese prince over 2,000 years ago, it is a food for millions of ordinary people nowadays, and widely found in Chinese and east Asian cuisines. Soy is a good source of plant protein for veggies. Get all the ingredients ready before you begin to cook the stir-fry as, once you start, you have to be quick.

SERVES 4

TAKES 15 minutes

Beancurd/tofu and mushroom stir-fry

- 2 cups / 200 g beancurd/tofu, diced
- 4 cups / 200 g mushrooms, sliced finely
- 3 stalks celery, cut into thin diagonal slices
- 6 scallions/spring onions, chopped finely
- 1 red or green bell pepper, sliced finely
- 1 cup / 240 ml water
- 1 tablespoon cornstarch/cornflour
- 2 tablespoons dry sherry
- 4 teaspoons dark soy sauce
- 2 teaspoons black bean sauce
- oil *
- water
- salt

* sesame oil is best

1 First, heat some oil in a wok and sauté the diced beancurd/tofu over a high heat for 2-3 minutes, stirring all the time, until light brown. Remove from the pan, drain on kitchen paper, and set to one side.

2 Now heat a little more oil in the wok and, when it is hot, add the mushrooms, celery, scallions/spring onions and bell pepper. Stir-fry for 2-3 minutes until the vegetables begin to soften.

3 Return the beancurd/tofu to the wok and toss it lightly to mix it in.

4 Taking a small bowl, combine the cornstarch/cornflour with the water to make a smooth paste. Then add the sherry, soy and black bean sauce.

5 Pour this over the mixture in the wok, and let it heat up while you stir until the liquid is bubbling and then cook for a further minute to let the flavors mingle. Serve at once with rice or noodles.

In this stew from **Chile** the pumpkin gives a slightly sweet taste which complements the tartness of the tomatoes and smokiness of the paprika. Pumpkins are fairly easy to grow at home. You can use your Halloween or Jack O'Lantern pumpkin for cooking afterwards – but ideally it is best to use the 'pie' pumpkin as it is sweeter and less fibrous.

SERVES
4-6

TAKES
45 minutes

Bean and pumpkin stew

V_a

3 cups / 450 g pumpkin, diced

1 can rosecoco or kidney beans, drained

1 cup / 150 g canned sweetcorn, drained

1½-2 tablespoons paprika

1 onion, chopped

4 tomatoes, chopped

2 teaspoons oregano

2 cups / 480 ml stock or water

2 cups / 225 g cheddar cheese, grated +

oil

salt and pepper

+ optional

1 Heat the oil in a large pan and cook the onion gently until it begins to soften. Now put in the paprika and stir round for a few seconds, taking care that it does not burn.

2 The pumpkin, tomatoes, oregano, seasoning and stock go in now. Stir, and bring the pan to the boil. Then reduce the heat and leave to simmer for 15 minutes. Stir from time to time until you have a thick sauce.

3 Now put in the beans and sweetcorn. Simmer gently for a further 10 minutes or so until the ingredients have cooked down, and then partially mash the stew with a fork. Serve with coconut rice or baked potatoes, topped with grated cheese and hot pepper sauce.

Nice with:

Coconut rice p42
Chutney p144

The demise of some of Tanzania's coconut palms has caused local anger. In *The Citizen* newspaper, HM Hussein berates Dar es Salaam's City Council for felling the trees for development, and says the council 'should remove the coconut tree symbol from its logo because there are no coconut palms to talk about in the city'. In the recipe here, coconut milk teams well with pinto beans, which are named for their speckled skin, like the pinto pony. It is delicious in soups and stews. The beans are often used to make refried beans and chili *con* or *sin carne*.

SERVES
4

TAKES
20 minutes

Beans with turmeric and coconut milk

v

- **2 cans rosecoco or pinto beans, drained**
- **1 can coconut milk**
- **2 tomatoes, chopped**
- **2 teaspoons turmeric**
- **4 cloves**
- **1 clove garlic, chopped finely**
- **2 tablespoons fresh cilantro/ coriander, chopped**
- **oil**
- **salt and pepper**

1 To begin, heat the oil in a saucepan and sauté the garlic. Then stir in the turmeric, add the cloves and cook for a further minute.

2 Next put in the beans, the tomatoes, half the cilantro/coriander, pepper and salt. Mix well.

3 Pour in the coconut milk and stir as the ingredients heat up – don't let the coconut milk boil. Top with the remaining cilantro/ coriander and serve with coconut rotis.

Goes with:

Rotis p132
Lettuce and raisin salad p94

What is now Syria lies in the Fertile Crescent, where settled agriculture first began. Eggplants/aubergines are grown there today. You can cultivate them at home but don't bank on a huge crop if you live somewhere with short, cool, unreliable summers... They give a good substantial feel to a dish, and take flavors well, especially cumin, as in this recipe.

SERVES
4

TAKES
30 minutes

Bell pepper with eggplants/ aubergines and tomatoes

v

1 green bell pepper, finely
  sliced

2 eggplants/aubergines,
  quartered and then sliced
  finely

1 onion, sliced finely

3 cloves garlic, crushed

6 tomatoes, chopped finely

¼ teaspoon chili powder

1 teaspoon ground cumin

2 tablespoons lemon juice

oil

salt and pepper

1 To begin, heat the oil in a wok or large pan and then fry the onion, bell pepper and eggplant/aubergine until they are softening.

2 Now add the garlic and stir-fry for a few seconds before putting in the tomatoes, chili powder and cumin and season with salt and pepper.

3 Stir the ingredients and cook very gently for 5-10 minutes, stirring frequently, to let the ingredients combine well. Sprinkle on some lemon juice before serving.

This is a dish from Zambia that can be a light meal or served as a casserole with mashed potato, rice or maize/corn bread. Black-eyed peas/beans are also called cowpeas and they're one of my favorite beans, with their mild taste and handsome looks. And I read somewhere that if you eat them on New Year's Day it is meant to bring good luck. Must remember that...

SERVES
4-6

TAKES
35 minutes

Black-eyed pea/bean soup

V

2 cans black-eyed peas/beans, drained
1 onion, chopped finely
1 can tomatoes, chopped
1 tablespoon tomato paste
½-1 teaspoon turmeric
½ teaspoon onion seeds
2 cups / 490 ml stock
oil
salt and pepper

1 In a good sized pan, heat the oil and then add the onion; cook for 5-10 minutes until it is golden. Add the turmeric and onion seeds and stir as you cook for a minute or so.

2 When ready, put in the tomato paste, tomatoes, stock, beans and seasoning, stirring well.

3 Add the stock and simmer for 20 minutes. If you like, you can partially mash the bean mix with a potato masher or fork, and then stir again before serving.

Try with:

Corn/maize bread p202
Walnut, cumin and sesame
nibbles p172

I generally use green cardamoms rather than black cardamoms which have a more pronounced flavor. In southern India, cardamom plants are common, and you can spot the aromatic pods growing out from the ground by the leaves.

SERVES
4

TAKES
40 minutes

Cardamom-flavored mushroom curry

v

8 cups / 400 g mushrooms, sliced finely

1 onion, sliced finely

3 cloves garlic, sliced

2-4 tomatoes, chopped

1 teaspoon fresh ginger, chopped finely

¼ fresh chili, de-seeded and sliced finely, or ¼ teaspoon chili powder

½ teaspoon ground cumin

seeds from 4 cardamom pods, crushed

1 teaspoon garam masala

1 tablespoon fresh cilantro/coriander, chopped

½ cup / 120 ml tomato juice or water

oil or ghee

salt

1 Start by heating the oil or ghee and cooking the onion until it is translucent. Then put in the garlic and the mushrooms and sauté these until they begin to soften.

2 After that, add the tomatoes, ginger, chili powder, cardamoms and garam masala, the cilantro/coriander leaves and salt. Stir these in well.

3 Finally, pour in the water or juice and cook gently for 5-10 minutes until the mushrooms are very soft. Serve with rice or chapatis.

Cashew nut trees in fruit are an intriguing sight in tropical areas of the world, including the Caribbean. The small pear-shaped fruits hang from the tree, and at the base protrudes the curl of the cashew 'nut', which is really a seed. Crunchy and sweet, this is a popular nut for use in both savory and sweet dishes (and for snacking too, but be careful – they are high in calories).

SERVES
2-4

TAKES
40 minutes

Cashew nut and pumpkin salad

v

2 cups / 300 g pumpkin cubes, boiled, drained and cooled
½ cup / 60 g cashew nuts, toasted
4 tablespoons oil
juice of ½-1 lemon
2 teaspoons liquid honey
1 tablespoon parsley, chopped
salt

1 Make a dressing with the oil, lemon juice, honey and salt.

2 Then place the pumpkin and most of the cashew nuts in a salad bowl, pour on the dressing and coat well.

3 Season and then scatter the remaining cashew nuts and parsley on top before serving.

Good with:

Couscous p48
Curried potatoes p64

30

'Ecuadorians love to eat meat but are very accommodating to vegetarian needs. If you head to a restaurant that doesn't have what you want on the menu, just ask and they'll be happy to put together a plate with beans,' writes Erin McNeaney on her Never Ending Voyage blog at neverendingvoyage.com. Or maybe they would serve a lentil dish, like this one.

SERVES 2-4

TAKES 30 minutes

Casserole with green lentils

v

1 cup / 200 g green lentils, cooked
2 cans tomatoes
1 green bell pepper, chopped finely
2 onions, chopped finely
1½ teaspoons ground cumin
1 tablespoon fresh parsley, chopped
1 tablespoon fresh cilantro/coriander, chopped
oil
salt and pepper

1 Heat the oil and sauté the onions with the bell pepper for 5 minutes. Then stir in the cumin, parsley and cilantro/coriander.

2 When they are all cooked and integrated, add the cooked lentils and the tomatoes with their liquid. Stir the mixture well.

3 Bring the pot to the boil and simmer very gently, stirring from time to time, for 10 minutes or until the stew is thick. Add water as required to make the consistency you prefer.

Goes with:

Marinated cabbage salad p96
Gingery mashed potato
with yogurt p78

One of the benefits of spinach is that it – or similar iron-rich dark leafy greens – is available pretty much anywhere. Spinach has a high nutritional value, including bone-healthy vitamin K and anti-inflammatory omega-3 fatty acids; it is also rich in antioxidants, especially when fresh, steamed, or quickly boiled. These Middle Eastern pastries can also be made just using the cheese or just with spinach.

MAKES
15-20

TAKES
45 minutes

Cheese and spinach pastries

½ **pound / 225 g filo sheets**

½ **pound / 225 g feta cheese, crumbled, or cottage cheese or ricotta**

1 **pound / 450 g spinach, chopped**

½ **teaspoon ground allspice**

¼ **teaspoon grated nutmeg**

2 **tablespoons fresh parsley, dill or fennel, or a mix of these, chopped**

melted butter or margarine

pepper

Heat oven to 350°F/180°C/Gas 4

1 Put the cheese into a bowl and combine it with the ground allspice, nutmeg, parsley, dill or fennel, using a fork to make a paste.

2 Cook the spinach in a very little water until it is soft. Drain it well, allow to cool and then squeeze out any excess water. Put it into the bowl with the cheese mixture and the pepper (feta cheese will not require any salt).

3 As you use them, cut each filo sheet into rectangular strips about 4 in/10 cm wide x 15 in/38 cm long. Keep the remaining sheets covered as they dry out very quickly and become brittle.

4 Put a little heap of the cheese and spinach mixture at one end of the pastry. Roll into a cigar shape, lightly brushing the other end of the strip with melted butter or margarine to seal. Fold in the sides to contain the filling.

5 Repeat this until you have used up the ingredients. Place the rolls on a baking sheet and bake for 30 minutes or so until they are crispy. Leave to cool slightly before serving.

Good with:

Cucumber salad p44
Classic rum punch p190

34

Fajitas are one of Mexico's wonderful range of tortilla-based delicacies. In this quick and tasty dish you can use red kidney beans, black beans, or pinto beans, and ready-made taco shells can be substituted for tortillas.

SERVES 4

TAKES 20 minutes

Chili bean fajitas

Va

1 can red kidney beans, black beans, or pinto beans, heated and drained

1 onion, chopped finely

2 cloves garlic, chopped

½ chili, de-seeded and chopped finely

4 tomatoes, chopped

½ green bell pepper, chopped finely

6 tortillas or 8 taco shells

2 tablespoons fresh cilantro/coriander or parsley, chopped

1 cup / 110 g cheddar cheese, grated +

1 tablespoon margarine

salt and pepper

+optional

Heat oven to 250°F/130°C/Gas ½

1 First heat the margarine and sauté the onion, adding the garlic, chili, tomatoes, bell pepper and half the cilantro/coriander once the onion is transparent. Cook gently for 5 minutes to make a pulpy, thick mixture.

2 While that is cooking, mash the beans with a little salt and pepper and then add them to the sauce. Mix well.

3 When almost ready to serve, divide the mixture among the tortillas, placing it along the center. Then roll up the tortilla and secure with a toothpick or small skewer. If using taco shells, follow packet instructions.

4 Place the tortillas or tacos in shallow dish. Serve at once with salad and topped with grated cheese, sour cream or yogurt, and the remaining cilantro/coriander.

Photo shows ingredients for fajitas

Kenya's cuisine can appear meat-heavy, but in fact there are many meatless dishes such as *irio* (sweetcorn, potatoes and peas or beans), especially at the coast, with its Arab/Swahili cooking. As one recent visitor noted: 'Meat is expensive in Kenya for locals, so if you are eating at a small local establishment, they will usually have lentils or the like.' Sweet potatoes, used here, have good fiber and vitamin content and can be made into both sweet and savory dishes.

**SERVES
4**

TAKES
40 minutes

Chilied sweet potatoes and tomatoes

v

**3 sweet potatoes, peeled
and left whole**
¼-½ teaspoon chili powder
3-4 tomatoes, sliced
oil and margarine
salt and pepper

1 To start, boil the whole sweet potatoes in water until they are soft – about 20-30 minutes, depending on their size. Drain and allow them to cool and then cut into very thin slices.

2 In a pan, heat the oil and margarine; add the chili powder, salt and pepper and mix well.

3 Now put in the potato slices and sauté them for about 5 minutes until golden brown on both sides. Then add the tomatoes and cook for a further 5 minutes, stirring. Serve at once, piping hot, with grated cheese on top if desired.

Goes with:

Corn/maize bread p202
Potato and bell peppers
with cumin p120

I liked this enthusiastic appreciation of the coconut on vegparadise.com: 'The coconut palm rates higher than the family cow to one third of the world's population. You can probably guess these people live in the tropical countries like Tanzania where the coconut tree is intertwined with life itself, from the food they eat to the beverages they drink. Household utensils, baskets, cooking oil, furniture, and cosmetics all come from the coconut tree. On the other hand, the uses of the family cow pale by comparison.' Coconut milk, pumpkin and sweet potatoes are a delicious mix in this recipe.

SERVES 4

TAKES 50 minutes

Coconut milk pumpkin

V

2 cups / 300 g pumpkin, peeled and diced

2 cups / 300g sweet potatoes, peeled and diced

1 onion, finely chopped juice of ½-1 lemon

4 cloves

1 cup / 200 ml coconut milk

½ teaspoon ground cinnamon

1 tablespoon fresh cilantro/coriander, chopped

oil

salt

1 In a heavy pan, heat the oil and then fry the onion until it is golden. Then add the pumpkin and sweet potato pieces and combine. Now pour in enough water to cover and cook until the vegetables are just tender, about 20 minutes – add more water if necessary.

2 After that, put in the lemon juice, cloves, cinnamon, salt and the coconut milk. Cover and simmer slowly for 10-15 minutes to complete the cooking of the vegetables, adding more coconut milk or plain milk if the mixture becomes too dry.

3 Adjust flavors and seasoning and then garnish with the cilantro/coriander leaves before serving.

Try with:

Cucumber and sesame seed salad p56
Mint tea p214

40

Rice is cultivated in over 100 countries, including Sierra Leone, and on every continent except Antarctica. You have to be pretty keen to grow it in temperate climates, but it can be done – check out Mother Earth (motherearthnews.com): 'If all you have is a sunny patio, you can still grow rice – in buckets. Granted, you won't reap a huge harvest, but it's a good activity to do with children and, if you choose an ornamental variety (like the purple-leaved cultivar Red Dragon) and an attractive container, it can even be decorative.' For this recipe, if you prefer your rice grains separated, see #1 below.

SERVES 4

TAKES 40 minutes

Coconut rice

V

1 cup / 200 g rice

1 onion, chopped

4 tomatoes, chopped

1 tablespoon tomato paste

¼-½ teaspoon chili powder

2½ cups / 600 ml stock

1 cup / 75 g shredded/ desiccated coconut

1 cup / 200 ml coconut milk

green stem of 1 scallion / spring onion, chopped

1 tablespoon butter or margarine +

oil

salt

+ optional

1 If you prefer your rice grains separated, cook the rice on its own first and fry the onion and tomatoes with the spices before adding them to the rice. Then put in the coconut and coconut milk. Alternatively go to #2 below.

2 Start by bringing the stock or water to the boil in a large pan.

3 Put in the onion, tomatoes, tomato paste, chili powder and salt.

4 Reduce the heat, cover and simmer for 10 minutes before adding the rice and butter or margarine, if using.

5 When the rice is in the pot, stir well and increase the heat to bring back to a vigorous boil. Then turn down to a gentle simmer and cook for 15 minutes or until the rice is almost done and the stock has mostly been absorbed.

6 Now shake in the desiccated coconut and mix it into the rice. Pour in the coconut milk and combine all the ingredients thoroughly. Cook very gently for a further 5 minutes, stirring frequently. Top with the chopped scallion/spring onion.

We grow cucumbers in the garden, and depending how hot the summer is (always a bit of a joke in Britain) we do get about 10 of the short, plump, hardy, slightly spiny-skinned Marketmore variety – which are delicious in salads like this. Sri Lanka's climate is kinder to cucumber cultivation.

SERVES 6

TAKES 30 minutes

Cool cucumber salad

v

3 cups / 300 g cucumber, sliced finely

1 teaspoon salt

½ cup / 120 ml water

1-2 teaspoons pepper

¼-½ green chili, de-seeded and sliced finely

2 red onions, sliced finely

juice of 1 orange

1 Start by putting the cucumber slices into a bowl. Then stir the salt into the water and pour this over the cucumber, mixing well and pressing the cucumber slices a little as you do it. Leave to soak for 20 minutes.

2 After this time, drain the cucumber and squeeze the water from the slices. Now add the other ingredients; mix well, chill before serving.

Delicious with:

Peppery potatoes with eggplant/aubergine p114
Groundnut/peanut stew p82

I love the delicate cilantro/coriander plants we grow in our garden, releasing their distinctive scent when I rub the leaves. We collect the seeds for cooking too. This attractive, colorful and simple dish from India goes well with almost anything.

**SERVES
4-6**

**TAKES
20 minutes**

Coriander carrots and potatoes

1 pound / 450 g potatoes, diced and parboiled

1 pound / 450 g carrots, diced and parboiled

1 teaspoon cumin seeds

1 teaspoon ground coriander

½ teaspoon turmeric

a little lemon juice

1 tablespoon fresh cilantro/coriander, chopped

oil

salt

1 To start, heat the oil and pop in the cumin seeds. Stir them round for a few seconds before putting the potatoes in, stirring as you do so.

2 Now add the ground coriander and turmeric and continue to cook on a medium heat for a minute, stirring continuously.

3 Put in the carrots, and turn down the heat to low. Give the mixture a good stir and then cover and simmer for 10 minutes to let the flavors integrate.

4 Check that the potatoes and carrots are ready; season and then squeeze on some lemon juice. Serve garnished with the cilantro/coriander leaves.

Try with:

Green lentil casserole p32
Yogurt and tahini dip p158

When we visited Morocco some years ago, we bought a couscoussier in the souk in Marrakech. You put the vegetables in the bottom and the couscous in the top part, and the veg flavors waft up to infuse the couscous as it cooks. It's easy to use an ordinary saucepan with a sieve to create the same effect. *Couscous* is often served with a sauce which includes the fiery *harissa*, a concentrate of chilis.

SERVES 4-6

TAKES 20 minutes

Couscous with mixed vegetables

v

1 pound / 450 g couscous
2 onions, chopped
2 cups / 200 g carrots, sliced
1 cup / 200 g pumpkin, squash or turnip, diced
½ teaspoon ginger
1 cup / 175 g peas and/or cooked garbanzos/chickpeas
3 zucchini/courgettes, diced
1 eggplant/aubergine, diced
1 cup / 100 g raisins or sultanas
4 tomatoes, chopped
½ teaspoon chili powder
2 teaspoons paprika
2 tablespoons fresh cilantro/coriander or parsley, chopped
1-2 teaspoons harissa *
stock
oil
salt and pepper

* or substitute 1 tablespoon paprika mixed with 1 teaspoon of chili powder and 2 teaspoons of ground allspice.

1 Use a saucepan which will be deep enough to sit a sieve containing the couscous across the top without it touching the vegetables.

2 Put the onions, carrots and pumpkin, squash or turnip into the pan first, as these take longer to cook. Cover them with stock and a little oil, ginger and pepper and simmer for 20 minutes.

3 Add more stock as necessary – there should be plenty of broth – and then add the peas or garbanzos/chickpeas, zucchini/courgettes, eggplant/aubergine, raisins or sultanas, tomatoes, chili powder, paprika, cilantro/coriander or parsley and stir well.

4 Now put the couscous into the sieve and rest this across the top of the pan. Place the saucepan lid above it and steam for 15 minutes or as necessary – many varieties are pre-cooked, so follow the packet instructions. If you choose to cook the couscous in a separate pan, just part-cook it and then transfer to the sieve so that it can imbibe the vegetable flavor from the steam as it and the vegetables finish cooking.

5 For the sauce, remove 4-6 tablespoons of the broth and put in a bowl. Stir in 1-2 teaspoons of harissa (or the substitute paste mixture) and mix well. Hand round the sauce separately.

6 When ready to serve, pile the couscous grains in a bowl and make a well in the center. Fill with the vegetable mix. Serve with yogurt and tomato salad.

Eggplants/aubergines are one of the most economically important vegetable crops in the Philippines. There are many different varieties; the type we've grown at home in Britain produces one or two mature fruits if we are blessed with sun and warmth. But it's great to see them, however tiny they are... and to cook them into a dish like this one.

SERVES 4-6

TAKES
10 minutes
+ 1 hour

Cracked peppercorn and eggplant/ aubergine salad

v

- 2 eggplants/aubergines, sliced, quartered and then sliced finely
- 3 tomatoes, diced finely
- 1 scallion/spring onion, chopped finely
- ½ tablespoon black peppercorns, crushed
- 2 tablespoons white wine vinegar
- ½ cup / 100 ml coconut milk
- 2 tablespoon fresh cilantro/ coriander, chopped

salt

1 Place the tomatoes, scallion/spring onion, peppercorns, half the cilantro/coriander and vinegar into a bowl and mix well. Set aside for half an hour.

2 When ready to make the salad, sauté the eggplant/aubergine slices until they are soft. Drain them on a paper towel to remove excess oil.

3 Place the pieces in a salad bowl and cover them with the tomato mixture. Set aside for 30 minutes.

4 When ready to serve, pour the coconut milk over the salad; season and toss the ingredients lightly to mix well. Scatter the remaining cilantro/ coriander on top.

Nice with:

Chili bean fajitas p36
Coconut rice p42
Mint tea p214

The fewer the ingredients, the better the yogurt. Ideally it would just be live culture and milk/soy milk, giving calcium and B vitamins. At home, we use it in many dishes – to marinate, to thicken sauces, or beaten into mashed potato and dips. This light, creamy dip from the Middle East has a lovely warm orange color.

SERVES 4-6

TAKES 10 minutes

Creamy carrot and yogurt dip

Va

2 cups / 200 g carrots, sliced thinly

⅔ cup / 150 ml yogurt

¼ teaspoon cinnamon

¼ teaspoon nutmeg

1 tablespoon fresh mint or parsley, chopped

salt and pepper

1 Begin by boiling the carrot slices for 10 minutes or until they are tender; drain well and leave to cool a little.

2 Now put the carrots and yogurt together with the cinnamon, nutmeg and seasoning into a blender and whiz until smooth.

3 Chill before serving with the mint or parsley scattered on top.

Goes well with:

Sautéed eggplants/aubergines in chili-bean sauce p136

Minted tomato and cucumber salad p102

Gambia relies, too heavily perhaps, on its groundnut/peanut exports to earn foreign income. In this recipe, the peanut flavor is piqued by chili to make a hot and bland mix; add lemon juice to produce a slightly sour flavor – use peanut oil if you can as it takes the high temperature without burning.

SERVES
2-4

TAKES
30 minutes

Crunchy peanut butter spinach

V

- 1 pound / 450 g spinach or other greens, chopped
- 1 tablespoon peanut or other vegetable oil
- 2 onions, chopped finely
- 2 cloves garlic, crushed
- 12 black peppercorns, crushed
- juice of 1 lemon
- 1 cup / 240 ml stock
- a few splashes of tabasco sauce, or ¼ teaspoon chili powder
- 1-2 tablespoons crunchy peanut butter
- oil
- salt and pepper

1 Using a large pan, heat the oil and soften the onions in it. Add the garlic and crushed peppercorns and cook for 3 minutes, stirring.

2 After this, put in the spinach, lemon juice, half the stock, tabasco sauce or chili powder, salt and pepper and then simmer gently until the greens have wilted.

3 Put the peanut butter into a bowl and gradually stir in the remaining stock, and then add this mixture to the cooking pot. Combine well and continue cooking for few minutes.

Nice with:

Rotis with coconut p132
Coriander carrots and potatoes p46

This sounds great – from **Cambodia**'s Peri-Urban Agricultural Centre: 'Organic veggies delivered, or you can order and collect at this warehouse location in the afternoons. The current production amounts to 70 tons of chemical-free vegetables per year, 30 different kinds of high-value European leaf plants, aromatic plants, fruit plants, and some root plants.' Cucumbers, as in this recipe, are widely cultivated in Cambodia and no doubt would turn up in the veggie box.

SERVES 4-6

TAKES 20 minutes

Cucumber and sesame seed salad

1 large cucumber, peeled
½ cup / 120 ml white wine or cider vinegar
1 tablespoon sesame seeds
1 onion, sliced finely
2 cloves garlic, sliced finely
1 teaspoon turmeric
½ teaspoon sugar
oil *
salt

* sesame oil if possible

1 Start by cutting the cucumber into 2-in/5-cm pieces. Cut these again into slender slices.

2 Now put them into a pan with the vinegar and salt; add a little water barely to cover. Heat up and then simmer for a few minutes until the cucumber is slightly tender and transparent. Drain, keeping the liquid, and let the cucumber cool. Set aside.

3 Next, toast the sesame seeds in a dry pan until they begin to jump and turn golden. Then let them cool.

4 After this, heat a little oil in a pan and cook the onion and garlic without burning until they are golden brown.

5 Now pour in more oil as required, and add the turmeric, sugar, and half the drained vinegar liquid. Stir this over a gentle heat until the sugar is dissolved. Add the onion and garlic and heat them through.

6 Arrange the cucumber pieces in a salad bowl and pour over the dressing. Mix well and then scatter the sesame seeds on top. Serve warm or cold.

Dishes on following spread: Cucumber and sesame seed salad; Samosas; Chilied sweet potatoes and tomatoes; Stir-fried veg combo with beancurd/tofu; Mushrooms and ginger; Creamy carrot and yogurt dip.

'Cumin' is a popular name for Indian restaurants in the West. As the world's second most popular spice, after pepper, perhaps that's not surprising. The spice is often teamed with coriander to give a dry, aromatic flavor which blends well in this recipe with the sweetness of the carrots. It's important not to let the seeds catch.

SERVES
2-4

TAKES
10 minutes

Cumin carrots

V

½ pound / 225 g carrots, sliced very finely

1 teaspoon cumin seeds

1 teaspoon fresh ginger, grated

¼-½ fresh chili, de-seeded and chopped finely

1 teaspoon ground coriander

½ teaspoon turmeric

1 tablespoon fresh cilantro/ coriander, chopped

oil

salt

1 Heat the oil in a wok and, when it is hot, sprinkle in the cumin seeds and cook for a few seconds. Moderate the heat so they do not burn. Then add the ginger and chili; stir.

2 Now put in the carrot slices followed by the ground coriander, turmeric and salt. Stir briskly and coat the carrots. Then cover, reduce the heat and cook for 1-3 minutes or until the carrots are done. Serve with the cilantro/coriander leaves sprinkled on top.

Tastes good with:

Fennel, rice and spinach p74
Nutmeg potatoes p108
Lassi p210

In a nutshell – from the Veggie Malaysia website: 'Most vegetarian diets are generally lower than non-vegetarian diets in total fat, saturated fat and cholesterol. Studies have shown that vegetarians seem to have a lower risk of obesity, coronary heart disease, high blood pressure, diabetes mellitus and some forms of cancer.' This tasty curry makes good use of spices.

SERVES 4

TAKES 25 minutes

Curried eggplants/ aubergines

2 eggplants/aubergines, quartered and then sliced finely lengthwise

2 cloves garlic, crushed

4 scallions/spring onions, sliced

¼-½ green chili, de-seeded and sliced finely

1 teaspoon grated fresh ginger

1 teaspoon ground cumin

seeds from 3 cardamom pods, crushed

2 whole cardamom pods

1 teaspoon fennel seeds, crushed

1 cinnamon stick, or ½ teaspoon powdered cinnamon

2 teaspoons mild curry powder

1½ cups / 300 ml coconut milk

1 tablespoon fresh cilantro/ coriander, chopped

oil

salt

1 In a wok or large pan, heat up the oil and when it is hot quickly sauté the eggplants/ aubergines. Stir them round and when they are brown and soft, remove from the pan, place on kitchen towel to drain and cool.

2 Now, using the same oil (adding more if required), fry the scallions/spring onions for a few seconds.

3 When these are beginning to soften, put in the garlic, chili and ginger, frying everything together for 1 minute while you stir.

4 Then add the cumin, cardamom, fennel seeds, cinnamon, and curry powder. Stir-fry for 2-3 minutes before pouring on the coconut milk. Season with salt and then return the eggplants/aubergines and cook gently for 5 minutes until the mixture thickens.

We were still digging potatoes up this last February – made harder by the days of frost that had turned the ground to iron. Many gardeners grow potatoes in East Africa too, and this is a tasty way to use some of your main crop.

SERVES
4-6

TAKES
20 minutes

Curried potatoes

2 pounds / 1 kg potatoes, diced and parboiled

2 tomatoes, chopped

1 onion, chopped finely

4 cloves garlic, crushed

½ teaspoon turmeric

¼ teaspoon chili powder

½ teaspoon ground cinnamon

1 teaspoon crushed coriander seeds or ground coriander

2 teaspoons tomato paste

4 teaspoons lemon juice

2 tablespoons parsley, chopped

a little water

oil

salt

1 Sauté the onion first in hot oil. When it is beginning to turn golden, add the garlic and cook for 30 seconds.

2 Now shake in the turmeric, chili powder, cinnamon and cilantro/coriander seeds and cook for about 1 minute to blend their flavors into the onion and garlic.

3 When this is done, mix in the tomatoes, tomato paste, lemon juice, parsley and salt. Stir before adding the parboiled potatoes.

4 Combine the mixture well to distribute the sauce. Now add enough water to cover the base of the pan and then cook, covered, for 10 minutes or until the potatoes are tender and the liquid almost all absorbed.

If you have some left-over dates, or nuts that are getting more wizened, don't put them in the compost... we quite often have dates, nuts and blue cheese like stilton or dolcelatte around for December's festivities, and this Mediterranean/North African-style snack is a good alternative way to serve them.

MAKES
12

TAKES
10 minutes

Date, cheese and walnut taster

12 fresh dates, or use boxed ones

12 slices creamy blue cheese, such as dolcelatte

12 walnut halves or pieces of walnut

Slice the dates almost in half and remove the stones. Open out the dates to make them flat. Arrange them on a plate and then put on the slices of cheese topped by the walnuts.

Serve with:

Couscous p48
Green lentil dhal p80
Pineapple and avocado salad p116

Pimientos, used in this recipe from **Uruguay**, look like red bell peppers but are a different variety and taper in shape. They are usually sold in jars, ready cooked. The rich red dressing is like a *sambal* or relish and in addition to being served with this dish, it makes a refreshing accompaniment to tacos or can be used as a dip in its own right.

SERVES 2-4

TAKES 20 minutes

Eggplants/ aubergines with pimiento dressing

Va

2 eggplants/aubergines, diced finely

1 clove garlic, crushed

1 tablespoon lime or lemon juice

1 scallion/spring onion, chopped

1 stick celery, chopped very finely

a few lettuce leaves

salt

For the dressing:

1 cup / 100 g pimientos, drained

1 tablespoon white wine vinegar

1 teaspoon mustard powder

¼ cup / 60 ml buttermilk or milk+

+ optional

1 To prepare the eggplants/aubergines, place the pieces in a pan and barely cover with water. Bring to the boil before adding the garlic, lime or lemon juice. Simmer for about 10 minutes until just tender and then drain well and set aside to cool.

2 While that is happening, make the dressing by putting the pimientos, vinegar and mustard powder into a blender and adding enough buttermilk or milk to make a smooth sauce.

3 Now mix the cooled eggplants/aubergines with the onion and celery, adding salt to taste. Place the lettuce leaves on a serving dish and spoon on the mixture. Cover with the dressing and serve.

4 Combine the mixture well to distribute the sauce. Now add enough water to cover the base of the pan and then cook, covered, for 10 minutes or until the potatoes are tender and the liquid almost all absorbed.

Serve with:

Curried potatoes p64
Kidney bean casserole p90

Growing avocados can be tricky unless you live in a nice warm place like parts of Australia and other tropical regions. In cooler climes they will grow in a heated greenhouse or indoors, but may not always produce the delicious creamy green fruit. In this recipe from the **Philippines**, the flavor of ground coriander gives a distinctive eastern note to this version of the classic Central American appetizer, guacamole.

SERVES 4-6

TAKES 10 minutes

Fragrant avocado dip

v

4 avocados

1-2 scallions/spring onions, sliced very finely

¼ fresh green chili, de-seeded and sliced very finely, or use ¼ teaspoon chili powder

2 cloves garlic, crushed

½ teaspoon ground coriander

1 tablespoon lime or lemon juice

¼ teaspoon paprika

salt

1 First slice the avocados in half and take out the stones. Scoop the pulp into a bowl and mash with a fork.

2 Now add the scallions/spring onions, chili and garlic. Mix well into the avocado.

3 When this is done, sprinkle in the coriander and lime or lemon juice. Season. Garnish with the paprika and serve at once with tortilla chips, carrot and celery sticks or slices of green bell pepper.

Delicious with:

Gingered bean curry p76
Mashed spicy
eggplant/aubergine p98

This simple dish gives a good range of protein, carbs, fiber, and color. The stir-fry cooking method, which originated in China, is great for whisking up a quick meal and a good way to use up left-overs, or veg that need eating. You don't need much oil and the fast cooking ensures that vegetables don't overcook.

SERVES
6

TAKES
20 minutes

Fried rice with beancurd/tofu

2 cups / 400 g beancurd/tofu, cut into small cubes

2 cups / 400 g rice, cooked and kept warm

8 cups / 400 g mushrooms, sliced finely

½ red bell pepper, chopped finely

6-8 scallions/spring onions, chopped finely

2 teaspoons fresh ginger, chopped finely or 1 teaspoon ground ginger

1 egg, beaten

1-2 tablespoons soy sauce

oil *

pepper and salt

* sesame oil if possible

1 Start by heating the oil in a wok and then cook the beancurd/tofu for 3 minutes, stirring all the time, until it is light brown all over.

2 When this is done, add the mushrooms, bell pepper, ginger, scallions/spring onions, rice, pepper and salt to taste, and cook gently for 10 minutes, stirring frequently.

3 Make a well in the rice mixture and pour in the beaten egg. Let it cook until set in the heat of the rice and then break it up with a fork and distribute it through the rice mixture.

4 Finally, splash in the soy sauce and mix this in to distribute the flavor before serving.

It's easy to overlook humble 'greens' in all their manifestations – spinach, collards, kale, amaranth, or sukuma wiki in Kenya – though perhaps some of the colorful chards are more remarked. But I love them and appreciate their low-key look that disguises their high performance on the nutrition front.

SERVES
4

TAKES
30 minutes

Fennel, rice and spinach dish

V

1 pound / 450 g spinach or greens, chopped finely

1 onion, sliced finely

1 cup / 200 g rice, rinsed

3½ cups / 650 ml stock

4 tomatoes, chopped + 2 tomatoes, sliced

1 tablespoon fresh fennel leaves, chopped or 1 teaspoon dried

oil

salt and pepper

1 Heat the oil in a large pan and sauté the onion until it is soft and golden. Add the rice, stir round and fry for 1 minute.

2 Next pour in the stock and stir. Put the lid on the pan, bring to the boil, and then simmer the rice for 10 minutes.

3 Now add the spinach; cover, and bring back to the boil. Reduce the heat and cook gently until most of the liquid is absorbed, about 20 minutes.

4 Next, put in the chopped tomatoes and fennel and combine these with the other ingredients. Cover and cook gently until all the moisture is absorbed and the rice is ready.

5 Season and then serve, decorated with the sliced tomatoes.

Good with:

Ginger beer p216
Nutmeg potatoes p108

I didn't really appreciate beans as a kid – aside from baked beans, which were a mainstay in my Cowboys and Indians phase, when I re-enacted campfire meals after going riding on a Saturday. I certainly didn't appreciate how important they are for feeding the world, including East Africa. I like these rosecoco or borlotti beans with their pretty streaked skins.

SERVES
4

TAKES
20 minutes

Gingered bean curry

v

2 cans rosecoco/borlotti beans, drained

1 onion, chopped

3 cloves garlic, crushed

½ green chili, de-seeded and chopped finely

1 teaspoon fresh ginger, grated

1 teaspoon turmeric

1 teaspoon ground coriander

1 cup / 200 ml coconut milk

oil

salt

1 First fry the onion in hot oil until it is translucent, and then add the garlic, chili and ginger. Stir these ingredients and cook for a minute or two.

2 Next put in the turmeric and ground coriander and stir for a further 30 seconds.

3 Now spoon in the beans and mix them into the flavorings, crushing them a little with a fork or potato masher. When this is done, pour in the coconut milk, stirring as you do so. Season, cover and simmer at a low heat for 5-10 minutes or until the flavors are well blended.

There was an attractive nursery garden I visited once in Kochi, India. Inside the crumbling, hospitable walls nestled many chili plants with pods/fruit of different shapes and colors. Red chili gives color and pizzazz to this delicious dish – while the yogurt imparts a tangy intriguing aspect to the flavors.

SERVES
4

TAKES
20 minutes

Gingery mashed potato with yogurt

Va

1 pound / 450 g potatoes, boiled and mashed

½ fresh red chili, de-seeded and chopped finely

2 teaspoons fresh ginger, grated

1 cup / 240 ml yogurt

salt

Heat oven to 425°F/220°C/Gas 7

1 Mix the chili, ginger and salt into the mashed potato.

2 Now beat in the yogurt and mix all the ingredients well. Turn into an oven-proof dish and cook for 10-15 minutes or until lightly crispy and golden on top.

Try with:

Hot cabbage with mustard seeds p86
Mushrooms and ginger p106
Honeyed coriander tea p208

78

'Holy cow!' We are familiar with this animal's protected status in India. Here's how it came about, according to the religious epic, the *Mahabharata*: 'Cows are the refuge of all creatures. Cows are the embodiment of merit. Cows are sacred and blessed and are sanctifiers of all. One should never, even in one's heart, do an injury to cows. One should, indeed, always confer happiness on them.' So, leave them alone! For this recipe, the lentils do not need soaking before cooking; they take about 30 minutes to boil in an ordinary saucepan.

SERVES 4

TAKES 30 minutes

Green lentil dhal

1 cup / 200 g green lentils, cooked

1 onion, sliced

3 cloves garlic, crushed

½ cinnamon stick

1 teaspoon chili powder

5 cloves

1 teaspoon ground coriander

1 can tomatoes, chopped

1 tablespoon fresh cilantro/coriander, chopped

oil or ghee

salt

1 Heat the oil or ghee and then sauté the onion. When it begins to turn golden, put in the garlic, followed by the cinnamon stick, chili powder, cloves and coriander. Stir-fry for 1 minute or so.

2 Next add the cooked lentils and tomatoes. Integrate these with the onion and spices and then cover the pan and simmer slowly for 15-20 minutes to draw the flavors together. Top with fresh cilantro/coriander and serve with yogurt and rice.

Around 200 Ethiopian smallholder farmers are now growing peanuts in addition to their traditional crops in a program in the Misraq Hararghe area of the country. This peanut recipe is also good as a filling for tacos, especially when served with a cucumber salad. The richness of the peanuts is counterbalanced by the cool watery clarity of the cucumber.

SERVES 2

TAKES 20 minutes

Groundnut/ peanut stew

V

1 cup / 220 g chunky peanut butter

¼ cup / 25 g peanuts

1½ tablespoon tomato paste

1 onion, chopped finely

½ teaspoon ground mixed spice, or a mix of cinnamon and nutmeg

1 teaspoon thyme

1 teaspoon ground ginger

1 teaspoon paprika

1-2 teaspoons lemon or lime juice

2½ cups / 600 ml water

4 tablespoons margarine or oil

1 tablespoon fresh parsley, chopped

pepper

1 To start the stew, toast the peanuts in a frying pan, without any oil or fat. Shake frequently so that they do not burn. Set aside.

2 Now heat the margarine in a pan and cook the onion for about 5 minutes until it begins to turn golden. Then add the tomato paste, thyme, mixed spices and paprika, pepper and salt. Stir well to combine the ingredients.

3 When the onion is cooked, remove the pan from the heat and stir in the peanut butter and enough of the water to make a smoothish, thick sauce.

4 Now pour in the remaining liquid, stirring constantly. Add the lemon or lime juice, check the flavors and then let the mix heat through before serving, topped with the toasted peanuts and parsley, with naan, pita or rice and a cucumber salad.

Goes well with:

Cucumber salad p44
Avocado tacos p16

Red, green, black, white... lentils in their many forms are a key ingredient in my kitchen. Most cook really quickly, without soaking, and as pulses they are highly nutritious. They are widely used in the **Middle East**, in recipes like this soup.

SERVES
4-6

TAKES
25 minutes

Hearty lentil soup

v

3 cups / 300 g red lentils, cooked

1 onion, chopped finely

2 stalks celery with leaves, chopped finely

2 carrots, chopped finely

5 cups / 1 liter stock

1½ teaspoons ground cumin

½ teaspoon paprika

juice of 1-2 lemons

oil

salt and pepper

1 In a large pan, heat the oil and then sauté the onion, celery and carrots until they begin to soften.

2 After this, put in the cooked lentils and stock. Bring to the boil and then simmer gently for 5 minutes or so, until the vegetables and lentils are cooked through and the flavors have blended. Add more stock or water if/as necessary.

3 When ready, add the salt, pepper, cumin, paprika and lemon juice and mix well. If a smoother soup is required you can put the mixture into the blender, adding more liquid if you prefer a thinner soup. Heat through before serving. A slosh of natural yogurt makes a great topping.

Tastes good with:

Red pimiento and pine nuts p128
Bananas with hot and
sweet sauce p184

84

Many people are 'involuntary' vegetarians in that they would eat meat if they could but it is too expensive. Nonetheless, some people in heavy meat-eating countries are opting for meat-free dishes as a healthy alternative, especially given concerns about heart disease. This dish comes from Tanzania.

SERVES
4

TAKES
20 minutes

Hot cabbage with mustard seeds

v

2 cups / 200 g cabbage, chopped finely

1 onion, sliced finely

2 cloves garlic, sliced finely

1 teaspoon curry powder

1 teaspoon mustard seed

1 teaspoon fresh ginger, chopped finely

¼ green chili, de-seeded and chopped finely

2 tomatoes, chopped finely

a little water

oil

salt

1 To begin, heat the oil in a wok and fry the onion gently until it is transparent. Add the garlic, curry powder, mustard seed, ginger and chili and stir these ingredients together for 2 minutes over a gentle heat, to blend them.

2 When that is done, raise the heat, add the cabbage and fry for 3 minutes. Then put in the tomato. Stir-fry the mixture for 1 minute and then pour in a little water, cover, and cook over a low heat for 5 minutes or until the cabbage is cooked. Leave to cool a little before serving to temper the flavors.

Try with:

Tajine p160
Nutmeg potatoes p108

Senegal's cuisine is influenced by former colonizer France, as well as by traces of earlier Islamic culture. This tasty dish is quite hot. Use turnip or swede/rutabaga if you cannot find pumpkin, and ginger makes an acceptable alternative to chili if you prefer a less hot but still spicy flavor.

**SERVES
6-8**

**TAKES
60 minutes**

Hotpot with mixed vegetables

v

1 pound / 450 g potatoes, chopped

1 turnip, chopped

2 cups / 400 g pumpkin or butternut squash, diced

2 carrots, sliced

1 cup / 100 g cabbage, sliced finely

1 cup / 100 g greens/ spinach, chopped

4-6 tomatoes, quartered

2 onions, finely chopped

1 chili, de-seeded and left whole, or 1 teaspoon cayenne pepper

1 teaspoon ginger

4 tablespoons tomato paste

¾ cup / 175 g peanut butter

water

oil *

salt and pepper

* peanut oil is best

1 First heat the oil in a large pan or stew pot and then brown the onions, adding the chili/cayenne and ginger when the onions are soft. Cook for 2-3 minutes.

2 Next put in the potatoes, turnip pieces, pumpkin or butternut and carrots. Pour in water to cover, and cook the vegetables for 10-15 minutes until they are beginning to soften.

3 Now mix the tomato paste with some water to make a pouring consistency and add this to the vegetable pot. Cover, bring to the boil, then reduce the heat and simmer until the vegetables are nearly done, about 20 minutes.

4 At this point add the cabbage and other leafy vegetables, and the tomatoes, with more water if required. Season, and stir.

5 When cooked, remove some of the broth and mix it with the peanut butter in a bowl, to make a smooth paste. Put this back into the pot and stir well; simmer for another 10 minutes or until all the vegetables are done. Serve with rice or mashed sweet potatoes.

Vegetarian restaurants are on the up in Nairobi, Kenya's capital. Generally the food is Indian, as mainstream Kenyan restaurant food is fairly meat-orientated. This dish is delicious served with sweet potatoes.

SERVES
2-4

TAKES
30 minutes

Kidney bean casserole

V_a

2 cups / 300 g red kidney beans, cooked

1 onion, chopped

6 tomatoes, chopped

1 cup / 240 ml milk

2 tablespoons fresh parsley or cilantro/ coriander, chopped

oil, margarine or ghee

salt and pepper

1 To begin, heat the ghee or oil in a heavy saucepan and add the onion, letting it cook gently until it is golden. Then put in the tomatoes and cook for 2-3 minutes.

2 While they are cooking, mash the beans in a bowl with a fork or potato masher.

3 Now mix the beans into the onion and tomatoes and add 1 tablespoon of the parsley or cilantro/coriander. Gradually pour in enough milk to make this into a thick sauce and then return the mixture to the saucepan. Increase the heat and bring it to the boil, stirring so that it does not stick.

4 Next, lower the heat, cover the pan, and let the stew simmer very gently for 10-15 minutes, stirring frequently to prevent it catching. The sauce should be fairly thick, but add some water or stock if you wish.

5 Before you serve, add the seasoning and scatter the remaining parsley or cilantro/coriander garnish on top. Serve with rice or baked sweet potatoes.

Good with:

Sweet potato bhaji snack p154
Minted tomato and
cucumber salad p102

As part of a healthy vegetarian diet, or any diet really, we need to reduce our intake of sweet and fatty foods. These foods are low in nutrients and high in calories. Indian cuisine can be fatty and sweet, especially those lovely jelabis. But this dish is not going to do damage on that front. A squeeze of lemon juice adds a zing.

SERVES
4

TAKES
30 minutes

Lentil and garbanzo/chickpea curry

V

2 cups / 300 g garbanzos/ chickpeas, cooked

1 cup / 150 g red lentils, rinsed

2 onions, chopped

2 cloves garlic, crushed

1 teaspoon ground cumin

1 teaspoon turmeric

¼-½ green chili, de-seeded and chopped finely, or ½-1 teaspoon chili powder

2 tablespoons fresh cilantro/coriander, chopped

1 lemon, quartered

water

oil, margarine or ghee

salt and pepper

1 To begin, heat the oil or fat and sauté the onion until it is almost cooked. Then add the garlic and stir round to fry them together. When ready, remove half of the onion and garlic mix and set aside for later use.

2 Now add the cumin, turmeric, chili, 1 tablespoon of the cilantro/coriander, and seasoning, together with 2 tablespoons of water. Cook until the liquid has been taken up.

3 Next, put in the garbanzos/chickpeas and the lentils and mix well. Cover with boiling water and then reduce the heat and simmer for 10 minutes, stirring from time to time until everything is cooked through. Add more water as necessary.

4 When the mixture is ready, add seasoning, and then stir in the remaining cooked onion and garlic. Scatter the second tablespoon of cilantro/coriander on top and hand round the lemon quarters to squeeze over.

With the range of fresh fruit and vegetables on offer, there are healthy eating options in North Africa, such as this salad. But of course a lot of the produce is shipped or flown to northern Europe because it is ripe and ready earlier in the season on Africa's northern coast.

SERVES
4

TAKES
20 minutes

Lettuce and raisin salad

V

8 lettuce leaves, shredded finely
4 tomatoes, chopped finely
2 tablespoons fresh parsley, chopped
½ cup / 50 g raisins or sultanas
1 teaspoon paprika
1 teaspoon ground cumin
a few olives
vinegar
oil
salt and pepper

1 First make a dressing with the oil and vinegar; then add the paprika, cumin, salt and pepper.

2 Add the raisins or sultanas and set aside for 5 minutes to let the fruit absorb the flavors.

3 Place the lettuce and tomatoes in a salad bowl and then pour the dressing over and mix well. Scatter the olives on top and serve.

Good with:

Fried rice p72
Caraway and ginger tea p186

This sounds a fun place to eat in South Korea's capital Seoul – the Myonginga: 'Korean vegetarian will consist of tofu; probably *bibimbap* (vegetables on rice with an egg on top); a lot of tofu- and seaweed-based soups; savory thin pancakes with green onions and chili peppers; lots of side dishes (different kinds of *kimchi* and rice, seasoned seaweed, thin soups) and fried vegetable fritters' – see happycow.net/asia/south_korea/

For the recipe below, if you cannot obtain oriental or Chinese cabbage (pak choy), you could use white cabbage or Chinese lettuce (sui choy).

SERVES
4

TAKES
40 minutes

Marinated cabbage salad

V

1 tablespoon sesame seeds

7 cups / 200 g Chinese cabbage or equivalent, chopped finely

6 in / 15 cm cucumber, halved and cut into thin lengthwise sticks

1½ tablespoons sesame oil

2 teaspoons fresh ginger, chopped finely

½ tablespoon sugar

2 scallions/spring onions, chopped very finely

1½ tablespoons white wine vinegar

2 tablespoons light soy sauce

¼-½ fresh green chili, de-seeded and chopped finely, or ¼ teaspoon chili powder

1 To start, toast the sesame seeds in a dry pan until they are golden and beginning to pop about. Remove and leave to cool.

2 Now put the cucumber pieces, together with the Chinese cabbage and scallion/ spring onions, into a salad bowl.

3 Using a small bowl or cup, mix together the oil, ginger, sugar, vinegar, soy sauce, chili and sesame seeds. Pour this over the salad and stir well. You can serve it at once, or leave it to marinate for 30 minutes in the fridge, turning from time to time.

'McDonald's announced it's considering a more humane way of slaughtering its animals. You know, they fatten them up and then kill them. You know, the same thing they do to their customers, isn't it?'
— US comedian Jay Leno's take on McD's.

Thankfully, there are no McDonald's in Algeria (yet), phew. Just good local food like this dish.

SERVES 4

TAKES 40 minutes

Mashed spicy eggplant/aubergine

V

2 eggplants/aubergines
2 cloves garlic, crushed
½ teaspoon cayenne pepper or chili powder
1 teaspoon ground cumin
1 teaspoon paprika
1 tablespoon lemon juice
1 tablespoon fresh parsley, chopped
1 tomato, cut into wedges
oil
salt and pepper

Heat oven to 400°F/200°C/Gas 6

1 Put the eggplants/aubergines, whole, onto a baking tray and prick the skins. Bake for 20 minutes or until very soft. Set aside to cool.

2 Scoop out the flesh and chop it; then place in a bowl and mash with a fork. Add the garlic, cayenne or chili powder, cumin, half the paprika, lemon juice and seasoning. Mix well.

3 Now heat some oil in a heavy pan and cook the mashed eggplant/aubergine mix, stirring all the time until it has heated through and the mixture is dryish.

4 Transfer to a serving dish, sprinkle with the remaining paprika, the parsley and a few drops of oil. Decorate with the tomato wedges.

Dishes on following spread: Coriander carrots and potatoes; Tajine; Gingery mashed potato with yogurt; Tangy eggplant/aubergine dip; Hot cabbage with mustard seeds; Date, blue cheese and walnut taster.

It's hard to find non-meat places to eat in Egypt, although the cuisine does have bean and pulse dishes, such as koshary/kushari made with garbanzos/chickpeas, lentils and tomato sauce. As one blogger put it: 'To all those veggies out there... my wholehearted condolences!! Having lived here for close to 4 years, I am aware of the desperation that comes from not finding a vegetarian place to eat out.' Here's a simple salad that goes well with several dishes.

SERVES
2-4

TAKES
5 minutes

Minted tomato and cucumber salad

v

6 lettuce leaves, torn or shredded

4-6 tomatoes, diced

2 cups / 200 g cucumber, diced

1 tablespoon red onion, sliced finely

1 tablespoon fresh mint, chopped finely

lemon juice

oil

salt and pepper

1 In a salad bowl, mix together the salad leaves, tomatoes, cucumber, onion and mint.

2 Make the dressing with the oil and lemon juice, and season. Pour the dressing over the salad, toss lightly, and serve at once.

Serve with:

Mixed veg curry p104
Gingery mashed potatoes p78

The vinegar-sugar combination is common to several Goan dishes, some of which are very fiery and need these ingredients to soothe burning tongues. Vinegar is not widely used in other regional cuisines in India – its use in Goa may stem from the Portuguese influence in its former colony.

SERVES
4-6

TAKES
30 minutes

Mixed vegetable curry with coconut

2 cups / 200 g potatoes, diced, parboiled and drained

1 cup / 100 g cauliflower florets, chopped, parboiled and drained

1 onion, sliced

½ teaspoon fresh ginger, grated

2 cloves garlic, crushed

½ teaspoon black pepper

½ teaspoon ground cumin

1 teaspoon ground coriander

1 teaspoon turmeric

1 teaspoon sugar

1 green chili, de-seeded and chopped finely

2 tablespoons creamed coconut

1 tablespoon vinegar

2 cups / 490 ml water

½ tablespoon tamarind paste

salt

oil

1 Take a large pan or wok and heat the oil in it. Then fry the onion while stirring.

2 Now reduce the heat and add the ginger, garlic, pepper, cumin, coriander, turmeric, sugar and chili.

3 Mix these in well and then spoon in the creamed coconut followed by the vinegar.

4 Pour on the water and add the tamarind paste. Then, turning up the heat, bring the pan to the boil. Put in the potatoes and cauliflower. Simmer for 20 minutes or until everything is cooked (you may need to add some more water) and then serve with chapatis or rice.

Nothing is zingier than ginger fresh from the ground, as I discovered during a visit to Kerala, India, where the spice grows well in the tropical climate. The high-quality variety known as 'Cochin ginger' is less fibrous than other types, making it good for cooking a dish like this one.

SERVES
4

TAKES
10 minutes

Mushrooms and ginger

v

8 cups / 400 g mushrooms, sliced finely

3 tomatoes, chopped finely

½ teaspoon fresh ginger, chopped finely

¼ teaspoon turmeric

2 tablespoons fennel leaves, chopped *

¼ teaspoon chili powder

oil

salt

* or use fresh parsley, dill or cilantro/coriander

1 Heat the oil and when it is hot, slide in the mushroom slices. Stir as you fry them for 3 minutes until they are evenly soft and cooked.

2 Now add the tomato and sprinkle in the ginger, turmeric, half the fennel leaves and chili.

3 Mix well and season, and continue to cook until the tomato has integrated. Scatter the remaining fennel fronds on top before serving.

'Urban agriculture' or 'City farming' is an important way to boost food resources and is practiced in many towns and cities across the world. People in Ethiopia's capital, Addis Ababa, have been involved in vegetable producers' co-operatives for around 30 years, growing veg, like potatoes, along the city's river banks.

SERVES
6

TAKES
25 minutes

Nutmeg potatoes

V

1 pound / 450 g new/fingerling potatoes, diced

3 carrots, sliced thinly

6-8 cauliflower florets, chopped

1 onion, finely chopped

2 cloves garlic

1 teaspoon turmeric

1-2 teaspoons ground nutmeg

1 teaspoon ground cinnamon

½ inch / 1 cm fresh ginger, finely chopped

2 cloves

2-3 tablespoons margarine or ghee

salt and pepper

1 First, boil the sliced carrots and diced potatoes for 5 minutes or until they are just becoming tender.

2 Pop in the cauliflower florets and steam or boil together for another 4-6 minutes until all the vegetables are done. Drain well.

3 Next, in a large pan, heat the margarine or ghee and sauté the onion and garlic before adding the turmeric, nutmeg, cinnamon, ginger and cloves. Then mix in the vegetables, turning well to coat with the spices. Season, and cook gently for 6-8 minutes, stirring frequently.

This **North African** salad is easy to make, and you can vary the mix – try adding some sliced sun-dried tomatoes – and the spicing; use fresh chili, de-seeded and finely sliced for a more fiery version of this dish.

SERVES
4

TAKES
5 minutes

Olive salad

V

1 cup green olives, pitted
1 cup black olives, pitted
2 tablespoons parsley, chopped
1 teaspoon paprika
¼ teaspoon chili powder
½ teaspoon ground cumin
¼ teaspoon cumin seeds
1-2 cloves garlic, sliced very finely
juice of 1 lemon
oil

Place the olives in a serving bowl. Mix all the other ingredients and pour over the olives. Mix well and serve with hot breads.

Goes well with:

Spinach and potato
casserole p150
Sesame and paprika eggplants/
aubergines p140

I first encountered papaya/paw-paw when I visited Malaysia some years back – and was entranced. It's usually served at breakfast or as a dessert, so this is an interesting culinary twist. This curry from India has a pleasant color and the garam masala renders it aromatic rather than hot.

SERVES
4

TAKES
25 minutes

Papaya/paw-paw curry with garbanzos/chickpeas

v

2 cups / 200 g papaya/paw-paw, cubed, or use canned (drained)

2 cups / 300 g garbanzos/chickpeas, cooked

2 onions, sliced

1 cup / 240 ml coconut milk

½ green chili, de-seeded and chopped finely

½ teaspoon cumin

½ teaspoon garam masala

oil, margarine or ghee

salt and pepper

1 To make the curry, heat the oil, margarine or ghee in a saucepan and sauté the onions until they are golden.

2 Then add the chili, cumin, garam masala, pepper and salt and cook for 1 minute, stirring well. After this, put in the garbanzos/chickpeas and heat them through.

3 Then add the coconut milk and, if required, enough water to make a little sauce. Simmer gently.

4 Finally put in the papaya/paw-paw pieces, stir, and let them heat through before serving with plain boiled rice or chapatis.

Don't forget the:

Chutney p144
Coconut rotis p132

'The time has come when we should all be able to wash ourselves, dress, eat and live our daily lives without feeling remorse for the animal products that we may have used.'

— The Indonesian Vegan Society

Although the main staple eaten in Indonesia is rice, potatoes, as in this dish, are popular too.

SERVES 2-4

TAKES 30 minutes

Peppery potatoes with eggplant/aubergine

V

4 potatoes, diced and parboiled

1 eggplant/aubergine, quartered and then sliced thinly lengthwise

1 onion, sliced

¼-½ green chili, de-seeded and sliced finely

½ teaspoon mustard powder

½ teaspoon turmeric

½ teaspoon grated fresh ginger

oil

salt

1 To begin, heat the oil in a wok or frying pan and cook the onion until it is clear and soft.

2 After that put in the chili, mustard, turmeric and ginger and salt. Then add the partly cooked potatoes and eggplant/aubergine and lightly brown them all over, turning constantly to prevent them catching.

3 Add just enough water to come halfway up the vegetables, cover the pan and cook gently until the vegetables are tender and most of the liquid is absorbed.

When I read this post on Savvy Vegetarian's Facebook page, I thought this salad could be the answer: 'I was wondering if other vegans would agree that lunch is the most difficult meal of the day. There aren't many options that don't take prep time unless you have sandwiches and I don't want to do that every day because of the carbs in the bread. Any ideas for quick lunches?'

facebook.com/pages/Savvy-Vegetarian

This is a quick and colorful salad from Haiti. You can add cottage cheese (vegetarian) and/or cashew nuts (vegan).

SERVES 4

TAKES 10 minutes

Pineapple and avocado salad

v

4 slices fresh or canned pineapple

2 avocados

½-1 tablespoon lime or lemon juice

lettuce leaves

2 tablespoons cottage cheese +

1 tablespoon cashew nuts, chopped +

¼ teaspoon paprika

oil

salt and pepper

+ optional

1 Slice open the avocados and take out the stones. Remove the peel and dice the flesh into small chunks.

2 Cut the pineapple into small dice and put these together with the avocado pieces into a mixing bowl.

3 Whisk up the oil with lime or lemon juice and seasoning. Pour over the salad and mix well.

4 Arrange the lettuce leaves on a plate and spoon the avocado salad over. Top with the cottage cheese and cashew nuts, if using, and sprinkle on the paprika.

Serve with:

Lentil and garbanzo/chickpea curry p92

Corn/maize bread p202

Honeyed coriander tea p208

India was one of the earliest centers of vegetarian practice and philosophy. The diet was associated with ideas of nonviolence towards fellow creatures. Today, sadly, meat-eating is on the up as some people see it both as desirable and sometimes also as a way of expressing their affluence. Potatoes provide easy and quick meals and accompanying dishes. Jazzing them up with spices gives them a sparkle.

SERVES
2

TAKES
45 minutes

Piquant
potato fries/chips

v

4 potatoes, cut into french fry/chip shapes, and parboiled
½ teaspoon turmeric
1-2 cloves garlic, crushed
1 tablespoon sesame seeds, toasted
oil
salt

1 Heat some oil in a heavy-based pan and add the turmeric, salt and then the potatoes. Cook for 5 minutes, stirring round.

2 When the potatoes are nearly done, put in the crushed garlic and toasted sesame seeds. Stir well, and then serve.

Goes well with:

Curried eggplants/aubergines p62
Spinach and bell peppers p148
Coconut milk pumpkin p40

Alternative energy is key to combating climate change, but there are snags. For example, sunny Morocco is to be a site for a huge network of solar and windfarms across North Africa and the Middle East, to provide 15 per cent of Europe's electricity. Sounds good? Well, the NGO Germanwatch wants local people to benefit from the scheme. And the developers say, yes, energy will go first to meet the needs of the local population before being exported. But why am I not reassured by this?

SERVES 6

TAKES 20 minutes

Potato and bell peppers with cumin

2 pounds / 1 kg potatoes, diced and cooked

1 red or green bell pepper, sliced finely

2 cloves garlic, crushed

1 tablespoon ground cumin

¼ teaspoon cumin seeds

peel of ½ lemon, thinly sliced

2 tablespoons parsley, chopped

oil

salt and pepper

1 To start, heat the oil in a heavy pan and fry the bell pepper until it begins to soften. Then add the garlic, ground cumin and cumin seeds, and blend these by stirring as they cook.

2 Now add the potatoes and turn them round in the oil so that they brown on all sides.

3 When they are almost ready, sprinkle in the lemon peel and mix in with the other ingredients. Season.

4 Scatter the parsley on top just before serving, with yogurt to accompany the dish.

Miso, used here, is a fermented soybean paste made with barley. It has a long history in China and other countries in eastern Asia, being rich in protein and considered good for the digestion.

SERVES
2-3

TAKES
25 minutes

Potatoes with miso

V

1 pound / 450 g potatoes, cut into french fry/chip shape, and parboiled

1 tablespoon miso

2 scallions/spring onions or shallots, chopped

soy sauce

1 tablespoon oil

2 tablespoons melted margarine

Heat oven to 350°F/180°C/Gas 4

1 Mix the miso with the melted margarine in a bowl.

2 Then spoon the oil into an oven-proof dish which has a tight-fitting lid, and add the potato chips.

3 Pour the miso-margarine mixture over the potatoes and stir round gently to distribute the sauce.

4 Cover and bake for about 20 minutes or until the potatoes are tender. Shake or stir them now and again so they cook evenly. To serve, splash on the soy sauce and scatter the scallions/spring onions or shallots on top.

Nice with:

Mixed veg curry p104
Cumin carrots p60

Versatile pumpkin or squash can be used for this **Caribbean** curry. There are many varieties of pumpkin. But I read that in German there is only one word used for all these, while someone in Sydney, Australia, wrote on the Jamie Oliver forum: 'Pumpkins, and all other similar vegetables (like butternut squash), are called pumpkins in Australia. Squash we usually reserve for the small flattish patty pan vegetable that is like a deformed yellow zucchini/courgette.' Whatever they're called, they are popular in kitchens around the world.

SERVES
4-6

TAKES
40 minutes

Pumpkin
curry

v

3 cups / 450 g pumpkin, cut into small cubes

1 onion, chopped

1 teaspoon turmeric

¼-½ green chili, de-seeded and cut finely

5 cloves garlic, chopped

1 teaspoon ground ginger or ½ teaspoon fresh ginger, grated or chopped finely

5 cloves

2 tomatoes, chopped

1¼ cups / 300 ml coconut milk

2 tablespoons fresh cilantro/ coriander, chopped

oil

salt

1 First, boil the pumpkin pieces in a little water for 15 minutes or until they are tender. Drain.

2 Now heat the oil and put in the onion. Cook, stirring, until it is soft and then add the garlic, turmeric, chili, ginger, cloves and tomatoes. Mix these in and then simmer this for 5 minutes over a low heat, stirring all the time.

3 The pumpkin goes in now. Mix it in well with the spices and continue to cook on a low heat for 5 minutes.

4 Pour in the coconut milk and half the cilantro/ coriander; stir to blend, adding salt to taste. Heat through gently and top with the remaining cilantro/coriander.

Pumpkins, potatoes, corn/maize and beans are key components of the cuisine in Argentina and other South American countries. This thick soup has a lovely golden-orange color. It is a good winter warmer and tastes delicious.

SERVES
4

TAKES
30 minutes

Pumpkin or butternut squash soup

V

3 cups / 450 g pumpkin or butternut squash, diced

1 onion, sliced

2 cloves garlic, chopped

½-1 fresh chili, de-seeded and chopped finely

1 bayleaf

2 cups / 490 ml tomato juice

¾ cup / 200 ml stock

a little milk

1 tablespoon margarine

1 tablespoon fresh parsley, chopped

salt and pepper

1 First, melt the margarine in a large saucepan and sauté the onion until it is golden. Now put in the garlic, chili, bayleaf and pumpkin or squash. Stir well.

2 Pour in the tomato juice and stock next; bring to the boil. Allow to simmer, stirring from time to time, for 20 minutes or until the pumpkin has softened.

3 When ready, allow the soup to cool a little and remove the bayleaf. Then transfer the soup to a blender, adding a little milk if desired for a thinner mixture. Return to the pan, season and heat through before serving, with the parsley sprinkled on top.

Pimientos and bell peppers are a delight – they look lovely with their bright colors and eat well too with a crisp bite when raw, or a sultry richness when cooked. In this recipe from North Africa you could use red or yellow bell peppers instead of pimientos.

SERVES
2-4

TAKES
20 minutes

Red pimiento and pine nuts

V

4 pimientos or bell peppers, sliced lengthwise into thin strips

½ cup / 80 g pine nuts

2 cloves garlic, chopped

2 teaspoons or a few sprigs of rosemary

oil

salt and pepper

Heat oven to 375°F/190°C/Gas 5

1 Place the pimientos or bell pepper strips into a shallow oven dish, with the oil, and cook for 20 minutes until they start to soften. Stir.

2 Now put in the pine nuts, garlic and rosemary, and season. Continue to cook, stirring so that the nuts do not burn. Let the pimientos or bell peppers caramelize a little as this creates a delicious smoky flavor.

Goes well with:

Green lentil dhal p80
Date, cheese and
walnut taster p66
Mint tea p214

Malaysia has great cuisine and plenty of places for vegetarians. The Happy Cow website at happycow.net lists where you can find them and the sort of food they serve. It's a site for veggie travelers, really, and lists cafés and restaurants in most parts of the tourist world.
You can use almost any firm vegetable for this dish.

SERVES
4-6

TAKES
30 minutes

Rich lentil and potato dhal

v

2 cups / 220 g red lentils

2 potatoes, cut into chunks

2 carrots, sliced finely

1 onion, thinly sliced

½ green bell pepper, chopped

1 clove garlic, crushed or chopped finely

¼-½ red or green chili, de-seeded and sliced finely, or 1 teaspoon cayenne pepper/chili powder

1 teaspoon turmeric

1 teaspoon mustard seeds

2 tablespoons fresh cilantro/coriander, chopped

margarine, oil or ghee

lemon juice to taste

salt

To serve:

1 banana, sliced

mango chutney

To make raita:

½ cup / 110 ml yogurt

1 cup / 100 g cucumber, thinly sliced or grated

1 Put the lentils, the potatoes and carrots into a pan with water to cover, plus the salt and turmeric. Bring to the boil and then turn down the heat and cook until the ingredients are soft, about 15-20 minutes.

2 While this is cooking, melt the margarine, oil or ghee in a large pan and fry the onions, green pepper, garlic, chili, turmeric and mustard seeds for 5 minutes.

3 Add the lentil mixture to the onions and spices. Put in half the cilantro/coriander; stir. Cook gently until everything is done and the liquid is mostly absorbed. Pour on a little lemon juice if liked, top with the remaining cilantro/coriander and serve with rice and side dishes as desired. For the raita, pour the yogurt into a bowl and mix in the cucumber slices.

Sri Lanka has always been a country where quite a lot of local food, including rice and soybeans, cashews and spices, is grown on smallholdings; but, according to War on Want, this is now threatened by World Bank liberalization policies that will allow investors to land-grab. Rotis complement many dishes – you can keep some in the freezer so there's always a supply.

SERVES
6

TAKES
15 minutes

Rotis with coconut

v

2 cups / 250 g flour
2 cups / 150 g shredded/ desiccated coconut
¼ cup / 60 ml boiling water
a little ghee or margarine
salt

1 To begin, gently warm the flour in a pan over a low heat, shaking or stirring it around.

2 Then mix the flour with the coconut in a basin and add a little boiling water to make a thick paste.

3 Shape this mixture into balls the size of an egg and then flatten them out to a 4-in/10-cm disc.

4 Put a little ghee or margarine in a frying pan and cook the first roti on one side for about 1 minute, then turn it over and cook for a further minute. When it is done, remove it and keep warm while you repeat the process with the remaining rotis. Serve as soon as possible after cooking.

Great with:

Tangy eggplant/aubergine dip p162
Rich lentil and potato dhal p130

'Being vegetarian in Pakistan is highly suspect,' says Maryam Arif on pakistanpaindabad.blogspot.com. 'Pakistanis never learn to love their vegetables. Greens are usually seen to be a curse, a last resort, an enemy.' But many dishes are adaptable, like these samosas, which are great with a squeeze of lemon... and a cold beer.

MAKES
8

TAKES
20 minutes

Samosas

V

filo pastry sheets
1 potato, diced and cooked
1 carrot, diced and cooked
½ cup / 85 g peas, cooked
1 onion, chopped very finely
3 cloves garlic, crushed
½ teaspoon garam masala
½ teaspoon ground coriander
½ teaspoon cumin seeds
½ fresh chili, de-seeded and chopped finely, or ¼ teaspoon chili powder
2 tablespoons fresh cilantro/ coriander, chopped
1-2 lemons or limes, cut into quarters
oil *
salt and pepper

   *peanut oil is good

1 In a wok, heat some oil and sauté the onion. When soft, add the garlic. Next, shake in the garam masala, ground coriander, cumin seeds and chili, and stir well. Fry for 30 seconds or so.

2 Now add the potato, carrot, peas and 1 tablespoon of the cilantro/coriander. Season, and stir. Continue to stir as you cook the mixture for 5 minutes (add more oil or a little water if necessary). Leave to cool.

3 Cut the filo sheets into strips roughly 3 x 8 in/8 x 20 cm. Spoon a little of the filling onto the middle of each strip and then fold up to make a triangle. Seal the edges with a little water and press them.

4 Heat some more oil in the wok and, when hot, quickly fry the samosas until they are golden on all sides. Drain on kitchen paper and serve hot, with the remaining cilantro/coriander scattered on top, and the lime or lemon quarters alongside.

Goes well with:

Tahini and yogurt dip p158
Lettuce and raisin salad p94

This dish from **China** has hot, strong flavors and so is best served with a plain accompaniment such as boiled rice. By the way, don't forget to compost vegetable peelings to fertilize your plants. There's debate over whether you can compost non-meat cooked food — some say yes and others no. It may depend on how safely (away from rats and the like) you can compost. So if you are concerned then don't do it. I tend to follow this advice from GardenNet: 'Basically, if you are eating it, your compost can too.'

SERVES
4

TAKES
25 minutes

Sautéed eggplants/ aubergines in chili-bean sauce

V

2 eggplants/aubergines, diced finely
2 cloves garlic, sliced finely
2 teaspoons fresh ginger, sliced finely
4 scallions/spring onions, sliced
1 tablespoon soy sauce
1 teaspoon chili bean sauce
1 teaspoon brown bean sauce
1 teaspoon sugar
1½ cups / 360 ml water
oil
salt

1 Heat the oil in a wok or large pan and when it is hot tip in the eggplant/ aubergine cubes. Stir them round until soft and then put in the garlic, ginger and 2 scallions/spring onions, cooking for 1 minute or so.

2 Now add the soy sauce, bean sauces, the sugar and water. Simmer, covered, for 5-10 minutes and serve garnished with the remaining scallions/spring onions.

Bananas lend themselves to this type of fried snack. I remember the little red bananas in Malaysia cooked whole, and sizzlingly delicious as they were lifted out of the wok. This version from Kenya is quite spicy, with chili and ginger. Too hot to handle? Just leave out the chili. Peanut oil is best for high-temperature frying. If you prefer to bake rather than fry, see #5 below.

MAKES
20-30

TAKES
30 minutes

Savory banana snacks

4 bananas, mashed

½ onion, grated or chopped very finely

½ tomato, chopped very finely

¼-½ green chili, de-seeded and chopped very finely

1 teaspoon fresh ginger, grated

4 tablespoons flour

oil *

* peanut oil is best

1 Mix the mashed bananas with the onion, tomato, chili and ginger.

2 Sift the flour into a bowl and slowly add the water, stirring to make a thick, smooth paste.

3 Now spoon this into the banana and tomato mixture and combine well.

4 Pour enough oil into a wok to give a depth of 2-3 in/5-7 cm. When it is smoking hot, add the banana mixture a teaspoon at a time and fry until golden.

5 If you prefer not to fry, heat the oven to 300°F/150°C/Gas 2. Place dessertspoonfuls of the mix on a non-stick baking sheet and bake for 20 minutes until golden.

Try with:

Pumpkin/butternut soup p126
Lassi p210

Finding veggie food is easier now in South Africa – the most interesting is Indian cuisine (especially in Durban) but the upswing of cafés and restaurants elsewhere has led to some spectacular European veggie food, and some fresh interest in South African dishes too, although many of those are meat-based. The ubiquitous Greek salad is a safe bet, but in the rural areas it may be made from packaged or canned ingredients plus a lettuce leaf or two.

SERVES 4

TAKES 20 minutes

Sesame and paprika eggplants/ aubergines

V

2 eggplants/aubergines, diced finely

2 tablespoons sesame seeds

¼-½ teaspoon powdered asafetida *

1 teaspoon grated fresh ginger

½ teaspoon paprika

¼-½ green chili, de-seeded and chopped +

juice of ½-1 lemon or lime

2 tablespoons fresh cilantro/ coriander, chopped

oil

salt and pepper

* available from Indian food stores
+ optional

1 To begin, heat the oil in a large pan or wok, and then pop in the eggplant/aubergine cubes. Fry them quickly, stirring constantly, until they are soft. Remove, drain on kitchen paper and set aside.

2 Using more oil if required, put the sesame seeds in the pan and add the asafetida, ginger, paprika, chili if using, 1 tablespoon of cilantro/coriander, salt and pepper. Stir briskly to combine the spice mixture and cook for 30 seconds.

3 Now return the eggplant/aubergine cubes to the pan and stir in lemon or lime juice to your taste. Mix all the ingredients well and then cook, stirring, for a couple of minutes. Sprinkle with the remaining cilantro/coriander leaves before serving.

Dishes on following spread: Minted tomato and cucumber salad; Beans with turmeric and coconut milk; Red pimiento and pine nuts; Rotis with coconut; Cracked peppercorn and eggplant/aubergine salad; Piquant potato fries/chips.

India's range of chutneys goes well with lots of things, including bean or lentil stews and curries, and cheese dishes. This one uses apples and adds a piquancy to samosas and other dishes.

MAKES
6-7 Jars

TAKES
70 minutes

Spiced apple chutney

v

3 pounds / 1½ kg cooking apples, chopped

3¹/₃ cups / 750 g sugar

3 cups / 500 g raisins or sultanas

½ cup / 50 g walnuts, chopped

2 teaspoons mustard seeds

2 teaspoons ground ginger

1 teaspoon allspice

1 teaspoon coriander seeds

1 teaspoon salt

3 cups / 700 ml white wine or cider vinegar

2 slices lemon or lime

1 Put all the ingredients into a heavy pan. Bring to the boil, stirring now and again, then reduce the heat and simmer with the lid off. Stir all the time, for 30-40 minutes or until the mixture has mulched down and is thick.

2 Remove from the heat and leave to cool before transferring to sterile jam jars.

Goes well with:

Samosas p134
Cheese and spinach pastries p34

One reason people choose to be vegan is to preserve natural resources by making the best use of water and farm lands. Growing food for livestock to feed people is inefficient, and is heavy on water and land too. You can try a different mix of vegetables in this dish from Indonesia, and rice or rotis make a tasty accompaniment.

SERVES
4-6

TAKES
40 minutes

Spicy vegetables in coconut milk

V

2 cups / 200 g potatoes, diced

1 carrot, chopped finely

½ cup / 75 g green beans, sliced

1 cup / 100 g cabbage, shredded

1 cup / 50 g beansprouts

½ cup / 50 g cucumber, peeled and sliced

2 onions, sliced

1 teaspoon tamarind paste, crumbled

½ teaspoon fresh ginger, grated

2 teaspoons ground coriander

1½ cups / 300 ml coconut milk

2 cloves garlic, crushed

oil

salt

1 Start by boiling some water and cook the potatoes and carrot for 5 minutes. Then add the green beans and cabbage and cook for a further 3 minutes. Drain, retaining the water, and set aside.

2 Boil the retained water again, remove the pan from the heat and put in the beansprouts to soak for 2 minutes. Drain.

3 Now heat the oil in a wok and fry the onions until they are translucent. Next, put in the garlic and then the sliced cucumber, cooking these ingredients for 3-5 minutes.

4 While that is happening, mix the crumbled tamarind paste with the ginger, coriander, salt and coconut milk in a bowl.

5 Now pour the coconut milk mixture over the cucumber and onion in the wok. Stir and heat gently for about 5 minutes.

6 Finally, put in the cooked potatoes, carrot, cabbage and beansprouts. Season, and cook for a few minutes, stirring frequently, until the ingredients have integrated.

Groundnuts/peanuts, used in this recipe, are a main source of protein in the **Central African Republic**. A 'relish' such as this is often used as a sauce or side dish to complement other dishes with rice or potatoes or – in CAR – with cassava.

SERVES
6

TAKES
20 minutes

Spinach and bell peppers

V

2 pounds / 1 kg spinach, chopped

1 onion, chopped finely

2 tomatoes, sliced

1 green bell pepper, chopped finely

1 chili, de-seeded and chopped finely

4 tablespoons peanut butter

water

oil

salt

1 To begin, heat the oil in a heavy pan and sauté the onion until it is golden. After that, slide in the tomatoes and bell pepper. Cook for 3 minutes before adding the spinach, chili and salt. Mix the ingredients well and then cover and cook gently.

2 While that is happening, put the peanut butter into a bowl and add enough warm water to make a smooth, flowing paste. Spoon or pour this into the pan containing the spinach and stir well.

3 Continue to simmer the spinach mixture, covered, for 10 minutes, stirring frequently to prevent catching. Add more water if you need to.

Serve with:

Tabbouleh p156
Avocado tacos p16

Here's another easy dish from India's vast kitchen repertoire. Spinach first appeared in England and France in the 14th century, probably via Spain, and it quickly gained popularity because it appeared in early spring, when other vegetables were scarce.

SERVES
4-6

TAKES
20 minutes

Spinach and potato casserole

V_a

1 pound / 450 g potatoes, diced and parboiled

2 pounds / 1 kg spinach, chopped finely

1 onion, chopped finely

2 cloves garlic, chopped finely

½ green chili, de-seeded and chopped finely

½ teaspoon turmeric

½ teaspoon ground mixed spice

½ cup / 110 g curd or cottage cheese+

½ teaspoon mustard seeds

oil or ghee

salt

+ optional

1 Using a wok, heat the oil or ghee and then lightly fry the potatoes to golden brown. Remove and keep warm.

2 Next, using more oil or ghee as necessary, sizzle the onion until it begins to brown and then pop in the garlic and chili.

3 Now add the spinach, turmeric and ground mixed spice. Turn up the heat and then stir as the spinach cooks down, about 5 minutes.

4 After that put in the curd or cottage cheese, the potatoes, salt and mustard seeds. Stir and cook gently for a further 5-10 minutes until the spinach has crumpled and most of the liquid has evaporated.

'Why did the tofu cross the road?
To prove it wasn't chicken!'

Ok – groan – there are more like that on veganworldwidenews.blogspot.com Enjoy this crisp and crunchy stir-fry from China. You can find canned water chestnuts in Asian food stores.

SERVES
4-6

TAKES
20 minutes

Stir-fried veg combo with beancurd/tofu

v

2 cups / 200 g beancurd/tofu, diced and fried

4 scallions/spring onions, sliced finely (retain some of the green stems)

4 cups / 200 g mushrooms, sliced finely

¾ cup / 100 g celery, sliced finely

½ cup / 50 g water chestnuts, sliced finely

1-2 carrots, sliced very thinly

1 zucchini/courgette, sliced finely, or a few green beans, chopped

4 cups / 200 g beansprouts +

½ cup / 100 g garden peas (canned or frozen will do)

1 cup / 150 g Chinese or white cabbage, shredded

4 tablespoons water

1 tablespoon cornstarch/cornflour

2 tablespoons soy sauce

½ teaspoon sugar +

1 teaspoon fresh ginger, chopped finely, or 1 teaspoon ground ginger

oil

salt

+ optional

1 To start, heat the oil in a pan or wok and add the scallions/spring onions, ginger, mushrooms, celery, water chestnuts, carrots and zucchini/ courgette or green beans. Stir-fry these for 1-2 minutes.

2 Add the bean sprouts, if using, peas and cabbage and continue to cook for 2-3 minutes, stirring all the time.

3 Now mix the cornstarch/cornflour with the water and pour this in, then add the soy sauce, sugar, cooked beancurd/tofu and salt to taste. Stir to mix all the ingredients.

4 Simmer, covered, for 2 minutes and then remove the lid, turn up the heat and cook briskly for 1 minute. Garnish with the retained scallion/ spring onion tops and serve at once with rice.

This recipe from East Africa uses flour made from lentils, but if you can't find it in an Asian foodstore, then use wheat flour. I was told that bhaji is the term for a more substantial vegetable dish, while snacks like these are called bhajia. But everyone seems to call these bhajis so I'll stick to that. They are good with chutney.

MAKES 15

TAKES 10 minutes

Sweet potato bhaji snack

v

2 sweet potatoes, diced, cooked and drained

1 cup / 110 g lentil or wheat flour

½ onion, chopped very finely

1 fresh green chili, de-seeded and cut finely

3 cloves garlic, crushed

oil

salt

1 To begin, make sure the potatoes are well drained of excess liquid. Then mash them in a bowl before adding the onion, chili, garlic and salt.

2 Now shake in the flour, stirring all the time with a spoon to make a smooth mixture that holds together. Then shape into walnut-sized balls.

3 Using a wok or pan, heat enough oil (about 2-3 in/5-7 cm) to deep-fry the bhaji and cook for 2-3 minutes or until they are golden on all sides. Drain on a paper towel and serve sizzling hot.

Goes well with:

Chutney p144
Creamy carrot and yogurt dip p52
Granadilla/passion fruit cocktail p204

We are often advised to eat 'low' on the food chain, and raw plant ingredients are just about as low as you can go, making this delicious and colorful salad high on Brownie points. This Middle Eastern recipe uses couscous, but you can use bulgur instead.

SERVES
4

TAKES
20 minutes

Tabbouleh

V

½ cup uncooked couscous
4 tomatoes, diced
1 red onion, sliced finely
4 tablespoons fresh mint, chopped
5 tablespoons fresh parsley, chopped
juice of 2 lemons
1 cup / 100 g green and black olives
oil
salt and pepper

1 Cook the couscous according to packet instructions.

2 In a large salad bowl, put in the cooked couscous, tomatoes, onion, mint, and 4 tablespoons of the parsley. Mix well.

3 Make a dressing by whisking the oil with the lemon juice, and season with salt and pepper. Pour over the salad and mix well.

4 Before serving, put the olives and the remaining parsley on top.

Sesame seed paste – tahini – is rich in vitamins and minerals. It's widely used in **Sudan** and the region's cooking and is also delicious as a spread on toast or crackers.

SERVES
4-6

TAKES
5 minutes

Tahini and yogurt dip

V

⅔ **cup / 150 ml tahini**
⅔ **cup / 150 ml yogurt**
2-3 cloves garlic, crushed
juice of 1 lemon
¼ **teaspoon paprika**
1 teaspoon sesame seeds
1 tablespoon parsley, chopped finely
salt and pepper

1 Blend the crushed garlic with a little salt, then add the tahini and mix to create a paste.

2 Next, gradually add the yogurt and the lemon juice, beating to create a smooth, thick cream.

3 Season, and transfer the dip to a serving bowl. Scatter the parsley and sesame seeds on top. Decorate with a little paprika and serve with carrot and celery sticks, and strips of hot pita bread.

Tastes good with:

Mashed spicy
eggplant/aubergine p98
Coconut rotis p132

Tajine in Morocco is cooked slowly in an earthenware pot (also called a tajine) over a charcoal fire. The long gentle simmering time coaxes out the flavors to make a delicious meal.

SERVES
4-6

TAKES
50 minutes

Tajine

V

2 cups / 200 g black-eyed peas/ beans, cooked

1 pound / 450 g spinach, chopped

1 onion, chopped

1 red bell pepper, chopped

1 green bell pepper, chopped

4 tomatoes, chopped

2 tablespoons tomato paste

½ teaspoon cinnamon

½ teaspoon grated nutmeg

water or stock

oil

salt and pepper

1 Fry the onion in the oil until it is transparent. Then add the red and green bell peppers and cook until they soften after about 10 minutes.

2 Now put in the tomatoes, tomato paste, cinnamon and nutmeg and stir well.

3 Add the beans/peas, salt and pepper and stir them into the vegetable mixture. Cook for 5 minutes.

4 Now season with pepper and salt before placing the spinach on top; add a little water or stock and stew for 20 minutes with the lid on.

5 When ready, mix the ingredients and then serve with rice or potatoes.

Barbecues or *braaies* are popular in South Africa and non-meat eaters are finding that lots of veg and fruit taste great cooked on the coals. TV presenter Sanza Tshabalala said he likes to put 'spiced pineapple on the fire, other fruits and vegetables and a chili bean hot-pot.' I like to barbecue or braaie eggplant/aubergines sliced lengthwise. This dip will go well with grilled vegetables.

SERVES 4-6

TAKES 30 minutes

Tangy eggplant/ aubergine dip

v

2 eggplants/aubergines
2 tablespoons lemon juice
2 tablespoons yogurt
1 teaspoon oregano
2 cloves garlic
oil
salt and pepper

Heat oven to 400°F/200°C/Gas 6

1 To start, pierce the skins of the whole eggplants/ aubergines and place on a baking tray. Cook for 20-30 minutes or until soft, and then set aside to cool.

2 Now cut them in half, and scoop out the pulp into the blender container.

3 Pour in the lemon juice, yogurt, oregano, garlic, salt and pepper. Combine well; taste and adjust the flavors, adding a little oil to give the consistency you prefer.

4 Transfer to a dish and decorate with paprika and chopped cilantro/coriander or parsley.

Try with:

Samosas p134
Cumin carrots p60
Ginger beer p216

162

The US Global Service Corps operates in Tanzania and has a helpful website for its volunteers which includes FAQs like 'Will I get sick when I'm there?' and 'Is being a vegetarian or vegan a problem?' The answer to that one is no, Tanzanian families will look after you, although 'being vegetarian/vegan is a foreign concept to Tanzanians... the Tanzanian diet is full of vegetarian dishes that are healthy and delicious.' Good. And this simple salad makes an ideal accompaniment to bean dishes.

SERVES 4-6

TAKES 30 minutes

Tomato salad

v

4-6 tomatoes, diced finely
oil
lemon juice
¼ teaspoon cayenne pepper or chili powder
2 tablespoons fresh cilantro/coriander, chopped

1 Put the tomatoes in a salad bowl.

2 Mix the oil, lemon juice and cayenne or chili powder together thoroughly. Toss the tomatoes and 1 tablespoon of the cilantro/coriander in the dressing and let the salad marinate for 30 minutes or so at room temperature.

3 Serve topped with the remaining cilantro/coriander.

Good with:

Spinach and potato casserole p150
Coconut rice p42

If you are lucky enough to have a glut of tomatoes from your garden, then this soup is a great way to use some of the ripe ones, especially as you could freeze it and enjoy the summery taste on a cold winter's day. This soup from Thailand has an interesting blend of mild flavors (coconut, milk and bean-curd/tofu) and sharp ones (tomatoes, lemon and curry paste).

SERVES 6-8

TAKES 30 minutes

Tomato soup with beancurd/tofu

v

2 pounds / 1 kg tomatoes, chopped

2 cups / 300 g beancurd/tofu, diced finely

3 cups / 700 ml coconut milk

1 teaspoon red curry paste

2 tablespoons soy sauce

1 tablespoon lime or lemon juice

2-4 tablespoons fresh cilantro/ coriander, chopped

salt

1 Place the tomatoes in a blender and make a purée. Then transfer them into a saucepan.

2 Now mix in the coconut milk, curry paste, beancurd/tofu, soy sauce, lime or lemon juice and half the cilantro/coriander.

3 Over a gentle heat, bring to the boil and then reduce to a low simmer for 15-20 minutes. Adjust the seasoning and then sprinkle on the remaining cilantro/coriander before serving.

Tastes nice with:

Coconut rotis p132

I was impressed by the British-based Young Indian Vegetarians mission statement: 'The human race will reach the pinnacle of civilization when it extends the hand of friendship and compassion to the animal kingdom and returns to the healthy plant-based diet best suited to the moral and physical needs of our species, thus avoiding the related evils of animal exploitation, human starvation and environmental destruction.' 'Drumsticks' used here are not chicken – they are the pods from the drumstick tree, quite common in India. You can use whole green beans instead.

SERVES
2-4

TAKES
60 minutes

Vegetables in coconut milk

V

4 drumsticks, chopped *
2 sticks celery, chopped finely
1 cup / 175 g yam or sweet potato, diced
1 plantain/green banana, sliced **
8 ladies' fingers/okra
½ cup / 60 g peas
½ teaspoon turmeric
½ fresh green chili, de-seeded and sliced
½ teaspoon cumin seeds
½ teaspoon ground cumin
5 curry leaves
½ cup / 120 ml yogurt
1 cup / 200 ml coconut milk
oil
salt and pepper

* Bean-like pods, obtainable in some Indian stores. If you cannot find them use whole green beans.

** To peel the plantain, first cut off the ends. Cut the plantain in half and run a sharp knife through the skin. Peel off and discard the skin and then slice the plantain as required. Parboil the root or hard vegetables first to reduce cooking time.

1 In a wok, heat up a little water and mix in the turmeric powder. When it boils, add the drumsticks or beans, celery, yam or sweet potato and plantain and cook for 10 minutes.

2 Now add the ladies' fingers/okra and the peas and continue to cook for a further 10-20 minutes. Then drain, retaining the water.

3 While that is cooking, grind the sliced chili with the cumin seeds; then add a little coconut milk to make a paste.

4 Heat some oil in a pan and stir in the drained vegetables. Add the spice paste, cumin powder, yogurt, coconut milk and curry leaves. Season.

5 Cook very gently without boiling, stirring regularly so that it does not catch, until the ingredients have combined. If it seems too dry, or if you prefer a more liquid mixture, add some of the retained cooking water or more coconut milk.

Although China's carbon footprint is growing, on the food front it is way ahead of many countries because people eat a very wide range of foods (including meat products, it is true) meaning there is not much wasted. Worldwide it's a different picture: the UN's Food and Agriculture Organization says that about one third of the food produced for human consumption is wasted — that's about 13 billion tons per year. In this recipe you can add beancurd/tofu or cooked beans.

SERVES 2-4

TAKES 60 minutes

Vegetable stir-fry with ginger

4 cups / 450 g mixed vegetables, sliced or diced finely *

½ pound / 225 g Chinese or white cabbage, sliced finely

2 teaspoons fresh ginger, grated or chopped finely

2 cloves garlic, crushed, or chopped finely

1 point star anise or ½ teaspoon aniseed

2 tablespoons soy sauce

1 teaspoon cornstarch/cornflour mixed to a paste with 1 tablespoon water

½ cup / 120 ml hot water

oil **

salt

* Such as leeks, beansprouts, bell pepper, green beans, peas, scallions/spring onions and carrots.

** Sesame oil if possible.

1 Start by heating up the oil in a wok or frying pan. When it's hot, fry the ginger with the garlic and star anise or aniseed for a few seconds, stirring.

2 Next, put in the mixed vegetables, stir-frying briskly for 1 -2 minutes, adding the cabbage when the vegetables are softening.

3 Lower the heat to a gentle simmer and meanwhile, taking a small bowl, mix the soy sauce with the hot water and salt.

4 Now pour this mixture into the vegetables, stir and then cover the pan or wok and simmer for a few minutes until everything is cooked.

5 After that, sweep the vegetables to one side of the pan and spoon the cornstarch mix into the center. Stir until it thickens, then quickly toss the vegetables in it and serve at once.

Sesame seeds are used to garnish many dishes in the Middle East – they are high in unsaturated fats and calcium, and impart a rich and nutty flavor. At home, we always put them into the dough mix in the breadmaker.

Walnut, cumin and sesame nibbles

v

1 cup / 150 g walnuts, crushed finely *
½ cup / 50 g breadcrumbs
1 teaspoon ground cumin
1 tablespoon tahini paste
½ teaspoon cayenne or chili powder
½ cup / 50 g sesame seeds, toasted
a little olive oil
pinch of paprika
1 tablespoon fresh mint, finely chopped +
salt

* Rather than a blender, crush in a mortar with a pestle or in a bowl using the end of a rolling pin

+ optional

1 The first thing is to make a mixture of the crushed walnuts, breadcrumbs and cumin. Put them into a bowl, and sprinkle in the cayenne or chili powder, salt and pepper. Then add enough tahini to make a paste that sticks together.

2 Shake the toasted sesame seeds onto a plate. Grease your fingers with olive oil and take up small lumps of the paste, shaping them into walnut-sized balls by rolling them between your palms. Then trail them in the sesame seeds to coat.

3 Before serving, arrange the walnut balls on a plate and sprinkle the paprika and mint over them.

Goes well with:

Melon and kiwi fruit daiquiri p212
Cashew and pumpkin salad p30

This potent dip uses walnuts, cumin and pomegranate juice – all ingredients common in Syria. The dip goes well with other dishes too, and can also be spread on warm bread. You can use lemon juice instead of pomegranate juice.

SERVES
4

TAKES
5 minutes

Walnut dip with cumin

V

1 cup / 125 g walnuts, ground
1 teaspoon ground cumin
1 teaspoon ground allspice
¼ teaspoon chili powder
2 tablespoons pomegranate juice
2 tablespoons dried breadcrumbs
4 tablespoons water
2 tablespoons oil
salt and pepper

Put all the ingredients into a bowl or blender and add a little water and oil as required to make the consistency for a dip.

Tasty with:

Cardamom mushroom
curry p28
Coconut milk pumpkin p40

The world of the web led 'Green thumb', a blogger in Uttar Pradesh, India, to purchase seeds online for the first time (indigarden.blogspot. com). She now grows broccoli, 'a wonderfully nutritious vegetable which is remarkably absent from Indian culture and cuisine'. Growing seed from elsewhere is kinder to the planet in foodmile terms than importing the mature fruit or veg – but it is best to go for plants that grow naturally in your area as these will be more tolerant of local conditions and therefore need fewer inputs such as water or heating. This is a lovely, quick and easy recipe that complements curries and other dishes.

SERVES 2-4

TAKES 10 minutes

Yogurt piqued with mustard seeds and tomatoes

V$_a$

1 cup / 220 ml yogurt
6 tomatoes, sliced
2 teaspoons mustard seeds
oil
salt

1 Heat the oil and lightly toast the mustard seeds for a few seconds, stirring.

2 Now add the tomatoes and mix them in well with the mustard seeds as they cook for 3-5 minutes.

3 Over a low flame, stir the yogurt into the tomato mixture; heat through gently without boiling and serve warm.

Try with:

Gingered bean curry p76
Spinach and bell peppers p148

Chile's *feria* or outdoor markets display an abundance of fruit and vegetables. Veggies can also head for the little natural food stores, the *tostadurías* that sell dried fruits and nuts, soy meat, and quinoa – the Andean grain with lots of protein. This mix has a really fresh taste with plenty of bite. I particularly like it in the second option below, where the mix is warmed on bread in the oven.

**SERVES
2**

TAKES
**5 minutes
+
10 minutes**

Zesty tomato topping

v

4 tomatoes, chopped finely

1 onion, chopped finely

**¼-½ green chili, de-seeded and sliced
finely**

1 tablespoon olive oil

1 tablespoon fresh parsley, chopped

½ tablespoon fresh mint, chopped

**warm bread, such as baguette or
focaccia**

salt

1 Simply mix all the ingredients together in a bowl, and then spoon onto the warm bread.

2 Alternatively, you can spoon the mixture onto the warm bread and then heat them together for 5 minutes or so.

Dishes on following spread: Lassi yogurt drink; Fudge with banana; Mint tea; Melon and kiwi fruit daiquiri; Date and walnut delights; Spicy baked bananas.

This **Caribbean** recipe is a lovely way to use up any bananas. And the skins are good for the garden: they contain nutrients like potassium and phosphorus, plus magnesium, sulfur, calcium and nitrogen. If you are a rose-grower, try burying chopped banana peel under the plants – it's meant to work wonders so I'm going to try it.

TAKES
70 minutes

Banana bread

V_a

2 bananas, mashed

½ pound / 225 g self-rising flour

½ cup / 100 g brown sugar

½ cup / 55 g raisins or sultanas

½ teaspoon grated nutmeg

½ teaspoon vanilla

2 eggs, beaten

½ cup / 85 g margarine

Heat oven to 350°F/180°C/Gas 4

1 First cream the margarine with the sugar and then add the beaten eggs.

2 Next put in the mashed bananas and the raisins or sultanas, the nutmeg and vanilla. Mix well.

3 Sift in the flour and baking powder, stirring to combine the ingredients.

4 Now spoon the mixture into a greased loaf pan/tin and bake for 40-50 minutes or until a skewer comes out clean. Leave in the pan/tin for 10 minutes before turning out onto a wire rack to cool.

Nice with:

Honeyed coriander tea p208

Bananas are grown in more than 100 tropical countries, including **Indonesia**, which produces around 55 million metric tons a year. This recipe teams the sweet fruit with a zing of chili to create a distinctive taste, but if the idea of chili does not appeal for a dessert, either omit it or serve the dish to accompany a savory meal such as curry.

Bananas with hot and sweet sauce

V

- 8 small or 4 big bananas, peeled
- 4 tablespoons lemon or lime juice
- 4 tablespoons runny honey
- ½ teaspoon allspice or cinnamon
- ½ red chili, de-seeded and chopped finely, or ½ teaspoon chili powder

1 First, mix all the ingredients, except the bananas, in a bowl.

2 Thread the bananas lengthwise onto skewers and cook them over a charcoal barbecue or in the broiler/grill, turning constantly so they cook on all sides without burning.

3 Now let the bananas cool a little and then remove them from the skewers and either pour some sauce over them, or dip the bananas into the sauce as you eat.

Can serve with:

Green lentil dhal p80

India has the most non-meat eaters in the world, estimated at around 40 per cent or roughly 400 million of its population. It also produces and drinks more tea than any other country except China, and some of its top teas include Assam and Darjeeling.

4 CUPS

TAKES
10 minutes

Caraway and ginger tea

v

- **1 tablespoon caraway seeds**
- **2 in / 5 cm fresh ginger, peeled and sliced very finely**
- **2 teaspoons cumin seeds**
- **4 cloves**
- **2 cinnamon sticks**
- **8 pine nuts**
- **4 cups / 940 ml water**

1 Place all the ingredients, except the pine nuts, into a saucepan and bring to the boil. Simmer gently for 5 or so minutes.

2 Now divide the pine nuts between the cups and then pour the tea over.

Take your tea with:

Potato and bell peppers
with cumin p120
Chocolate rum cake p188

Baxter's Road in Bridgetown, capital of $\mathrm{Barbados}$, is a buzzy place to eat – open all hours. Barbadian delicacies are available from streetside vendors: fried fish, pudding, *souse* (a pork dish), peas and rice, *jug-jug* (a Christmas favorite made mainly of green peas and guinea corn), boiled corn... possibly even chocolate rum cake. And all to the background of loud calypso or reggae music.

**TAKES
70 minutes**

Chocolate rum cake

$\mathrm{V_a}$

1 tablespoon cocoa powder

½ cup / 110 g butter or margarine

1½ cups / 300 g brown sugar

2 eggs

1 cup / 110 g raisins

2½ cups / 275 g flour

2 teaspoons baking powder

½ teaspoon cinnamon

3 tablespoons water

½ cup / 100 ml buttermilk or milk

3 tablespoons rum

10 blanched almonds and/ or 5 strawberries, halved

Heat the oven to 350°F/180°C/Gas 4

1 Cream the butter and sugar until light and fluffy.

2 Separate the eggs and retain the whites. Add the egg yolks and raisins to the butter and sugar mix.

3 Now sift the flour together with the cocoa, baking powder, salt, and cinnamon and shake this into the mixture.

4 After that, pour in the water, buttermilk or milk and rum, and mix round.

5 Beat the egg whites until they are stiff and fold them in gently. Pour into a rectangular, greased pan/tin. Bake for about 50-60 minutes. Towards the end of the cooking time, place the almonds on top. When the cake is ready, leave it in the pan/tin for 10 minutes. Cool on a rack and decorate with the strawberries before serving.

Ernest Hemingway lived in Cuba with his then wife, the journalist and writer Martha Gellhorn. La Floridita bar in Havana was Hemingway's favorite cocktail haunt. This punch is particularly pleasing, with its addition of grated nutmeg complementing the lime juice. Try it also with mango or passion fruit (granadilla) juice.

2 GLASSES

TAKES
5 minutes

Classic rum punch

V

2 tablespoons lime juice
1 tablespoon superfine/caster sugar
½ teaspoon grated nutmeg
4 tablespoons orange or pineapple juice
dash of angostura bitters +
2-4 tablespoons rum

+ optional

Put all the ingredients into a blender and then serve over cracked ice.

Slurp this with:

Piquant potato fries/chips p118
Coconut rotis p132
Cheese and spinach pastries p34

A post on happycow.net about the Mavalli Tiffin Rooms reads: 'Vegetarian restaurant serving authentic Karnataka and South Indian dishes with vegan options.' Sounds tempting. 'Tiffin' is a word from British **India** days, with various meanings from light meal to lunch or snack. These sweetmeats would do for tiffin. They are lovely, and easy to make with the kids. Just keep a close watch over and stir the evaporated milk so it doesn't catch and burn.

MAKES
10-15
PIECES

TAKES
30 minutes

Coconut sweetmeats

V_a

¾ **cup / 180 ml evaporated milk**

1¼ **cups / 100 g shredded/desiccated coconut**

4 **teaspoons / 30 g sugar**

1 **cardamom pod**

1 First of all, pour the evaporated milk into a pan and add the sugar and the cardamom pod. Heat gently, stirring all the time. When it boils, turn down the heat and simmer, stirring frequently, until the milk has reduced by half.

2 Remove the pan from the heat and shake in the coconut. Stir to combine milk and coconut into a ball. Then remove from the pan and transfer to a greased shallow dish or toffee tray. Spread it evenly, using the back of a metal spoon.

3 Leave the mixture to cool and then cut into small pieces. It is best served at room temperature, so if you store it in the fridge take it out an hour or so before serving.

Good with:

Lassi p210

Apparently there are 95 commercial varieties of dates in Libya, with some fine names including Talis and Zebur. This tasty snack could be made more quickly in a food processor, but I prefer to chop the items so that they are not too smooth.

MAKES
15

TAKES
**30 minutes
+ 1 hour
in fridge**

Date and walnut delights

V

½ **pound / 225 g dates, pitted and chopped finely**

¼ **pound / 110 g figs, chopped finely**

1 **cup / 110 g walnuts, crushed ***

¼ **teaspoon ground aniseed**

¼ **teaspoon ground coriander**

½ **teaspoon ground allspice**

2 **teaspoons clear honey**

a few drops orange-blossom water +

***** One way to do this is to put the walnuts in a bowl and stamp them with the end of a rolling pin.

+ optional

1 Put the chopped dates and figs into a bowl and stir in the crushed walnuts. Mix well and then add the aniseed, coriander, allspice, honey, and the orange-blossom water, if using. Combine the ingredients well.

2 Then press the mixture into a small shallow dish or baking pan/tin. Chill for an hour and then cut into small squares to serve. You can store it for a week.

Algeria's cuisine is not generally meat-free but you can pick your way through and find vegetables, including tomatoes, olives, peppers, eggplant/aubergine, and lentils. Meals may end with fresh fruit and dates, perhaps baked into cookies like these.

MAKES
30-40

TAKES
45 minutes

Date cookies

V_a

1 cup / 250 g unsalted butter

1 cup / 125 g confectioner's/icing sugar

2½ cups / 300 g flour

20 dates, pitted

Heat oven to 300°F/150°C/Gas 2

1 Start by beating the butter and sugar together to produce a light, white mixture.

2 Now sieve in the flour and use your hands to incorporate it into the butter and sugar mix; it should be soft but not too sticky.

3 Flour your hands and take up bits of the dough to shape into small round balls. Place on a non-stick baking sheet, fairly far apart, and then press the balls flat.

4 Put half a date on each cookie and then bake for about 20-30 minutes until the cookies are golden.

Good with:

Mint tea p214
Caraway and ginger tea p186

The good: Bananas are very low in saturated fat, cholesterol and sodium. They are also a good source of fiber, vitamins C and B6; potassium and manganese. *The bad:* A large portion of the calories in bananas come from sugars. *The ugly:* Many exported ones are grown in a heavy haze of pesticides. Try to get Fair Trade and organic bananas. Sweetmeats like this one from South India are often given as gifts at Hindu festivals. This is pretty simple to make, and the banana and cardamom flavors complement each other well.

**MAKES
12**

**TAKES
15 minutes**

Fudge with banana

v

1 large banana
¼ cup / 50 g semolina
¼ cup / 50 g ground almonds
seeds from 3 cardamom pods, crushed
⅓ cup / 50 g sugar
1-2 teaspoons water
2 tablespoons margarine

1 To begin, put the banana into a bowl and mash it with a fork. Add the crushed cardamom seeds and mix well.

2 Now melt the margarine in a pan and gently cook the semolina, stirring, until it turns golden. When this is ready, add the banana mixture, ground almonds, sugar and a little water, taking care that it does not become too wet.

3 Bring to the boil and then reduce the heat and cook, stirring constantly, for 3-5 minutes or until the mixture comes away from the sides of the pan/tin.

4 Spoon it into a shallow greased pan/tin and let it cool a little. Press with the back of a metal spoon to smooth the surface and then put it into the fridge to set. Cut into small pieces or roll into balls to serve.

We used to eat McVitie's Jamaica ginger cake that came in a packet, and we'd put butter or more likely margarine on it. While that cake was pleasant enough, this one is much more punchy. Jamaica is the major world supplier of allspice, used in this tangy, moist cake.

TAKES
75 minutes

Ginger-hot gingerbread

1½ cups / 175 g self-rising flour

½ teaspoon allspice, ground

2 teaspoons ground ginger or fresh ginger, chopped, or 1 tablespoon preserved/stem ginger, chopped finely

2 tablespoons raisins or sultanas

½ cup / 100 g butter or margarine

⅓ cup / 60 g sugar

1 tablespoon molasses or black treacle

150 ml milk

2 eggs, beaten

1 tablespoon rum +

+ optional

Heat oven to 350°F/180°C/Gas 4

1 Start by sifting the flour into a bowl and add the allspice, ginger and raisins or sultanas.

2 Now melt the margarine or butter and put in the sugar and molasses or black treacle. Mix well and heat up to boiling point. Pour onto the flour and mix well.

3 When that is done, take a new bowl for the beaten eggs and mix the milk into them. Then add this, gradually, to the flour mixture, stirring as you do so.

4 Add the rum now, if using. Spoon the mixture into a greased 8 x 4 in/20 x 10 cm loaf pan/tin and bake for 45-60 minutes or until a skewer comes out clean. Leave in the pan/tin for 15 minutes and then turn out onto a wire rack to cool.

In Kibera, the huge slum area in Nairobi, Kenya, 'vertical cities' provide a novel way to boost food sources. Rice or maize sacks are filled with soil so that women with limited land can grow food like onions, spinach and tomatoes on multiple levels. This just-sweet maize bread goes well with some vegetable stews or curries. You can also eat it as a tea bread with jam or honey. It is slightly sweet and for me that also makes it delicious with some cheeses, such as stilton.

TAKES
40 minutes

Golden corn/ maize bread

²/₃ cup / 100 g cornmeal/ maize meal

1 cup / 125 g wholewheat flour

4 teaspoons baking soda

2 tablespoons sugar

1 egg, beaten

2 tablespoons/ 25 g margarine, melted

½ cup / 120 ml milk

pinch of salt

Heat oven to 350°F/180°C/Gas 4

1 First, sieve the flour and cornmeal/maize meal with the baking soda, salt and sugar into a bowl.

2 Now put in the beaten egg and melted margarine with enough milk to make a stiff mixture.

3 Stir well and then spoon the mix into a greased loaf or cake pan/tin. Spread the mixture evenly and then cook for 20-30 minutes. When it is ready, leave the bread to cool for a while before turning out of the pan/tin to serve.

I first tasted granadilla/passion fruit, used in this Sri Lankan drink, many years ago when it was in the exotic fruit section of the local supermarket. I dread to think how much fuel and money had gone into getting it to Britain. But nowadays it is quite commonly seen on fruit stalls and I must say I love its sour-sweet flavor. It's nice to know when sipping this delicious cocktail that passion fruit contain antioxidants, fiber, and vitamins A and C. So it could be construed as a sort-of healthy drink.

SERVES 2

TAKES 5 minutes

Granadilla/passion fruit cocktail

V

¼ cup / 60 ml dark rum
½ cup / 120 ml passion fruit or orange juice
2 teaspoons coconut milk
6 fresh strawberries
dash of lime or lemon juice

Keeping back 2 of the strawberries, simply blend the remaining ingredients together with crushed ice. Slice the 2 retained strawberries lengthwise, almost through but not completely so that you can sit them on the rim of the glasses before serving the cocktail.

Good with:

Walnut, cumin and sesame nibbles p172
Avocado dip p70

'There is more to Caribbean cooking than rice and beans, pineapples, coconut and tropical fruit,' says Taymer Mason on her Vegan in the Sun blog. She's right of course, but the fruit is wonderful. Here's an alcohol-free, fresh-tasting and refreshing drink that's perfect for a hot day. If possible, use limes, as they just have that extra something, that twist of mischief. You can sieve the juice before serving if you prefer.

MAKES
2 drinks

TAKES
10 minutes

Granadilla/ passion fruit juice

v

12 granadillas/passion
  fruits
1 cup / 240 ml water
juice of 2 limes or lemons
sugar to taste

1 Cut the fruit in half and spoon the pulp into a saucepan. Add the water and then bring gently to the boil.

2 Allow to cool a little before adding the lime or lemon juice and sugar. Stir well. Chill before serving.

Nice with:

Coconut sweetmeats p192

Here's a colorful tale. When Jordanian activist Amina Tariq took to the streets of Amman clad in lettuce leaves, she captured the attention of the Middle East's media. With a sign in Arabic that read 'Let vegetarianism grow on you', she was trying to spark interest in a diet without animal products. According to Hossam Gamal, a researcher at the Egyptian agriculture ministry, 'we could increase the health and living situation for millions of people if we didn't have to spend so much on maintaining the desire to eat meat'. After that, how about a nice cup of tea...

MAKES
1 cup

TAKES
5 minutes

Honeyed coriander tea

v

1 cup / 240 ml water
1 teaspoon ground coriander
½ teaspoon cinnamon
1-2 teaspoons honey
teabag

Put the spices and honey into the cup containing the tea and pour on the boiling water. Stir well, and leave to cool a little before drinking.

Good with:

Vegetable stir-fry
with ginger p170
Banana bread p182

Lassi, made from yogurt, is a common accompaniment to curry meals in **India**, but as it is so easy to make you can drink it any time as a change from other soft drinks. It's also delicious with fruit such as banana blended into it.

SERVES
4

TAKES
5 minutes

Lassi
yogurt drink

2 small cartons yogurt
2½ cups / 590 ml cold water
juice of ½ lemon
2 teaspoons sugar +
pinch of cinnamon for topping

+ a little salt can be used to flavor instead of sugar

Simply blend all ingredients until frothy and pour into glasses. Top with a sprinkle of cinnamon.

Good with:

Pumpkin curry p124
Zesty tomato topping p178
Avocado tacos p16

The **Caribbean**, with its bountiful fruits and abundance of rum, sun and beaches is the cocktail capital of the world. A daiquiri is usually made with rum, lime juice, sugar and some sweet fruit; it's also the name of a beach in Cuba.

SERVES
4

TAKES
10 minutes

Melon and kiwi fruit daiquiri

V

2 slices melon
3 kiwi fruit
juice of 1 lime
1 cup / 240 ml orange juice
1/3 cup / 100 ml rum
2 tablespoons superfine/
   caster sugar
ice cubes

1 Remove the flesh from the melon and chop. Peel 2 of the kiwi fruits and put them and the melon into a blender with the lime juice, orange juice, rum and sugar.

2 Whizz to mix, and then pour over crushed ice cubes. Cut the remaining kiwi fruit into slices to sit on the side of the cocktail glass, and/or on top of the cocktail.

People carrying trays of tea in little cups from café to shop or office is a common sight in parts of North Africa. This fragrant minty tea is good hot and you can keep any left over to serve cold as a refreshing lunchtime drink (see #2 below).

SERVES
2-4

TAKES
5 minutes

Mint tea

V

3 teabags
4 tablespoons mint leaves
1-2 tablespoons sugar +
water

+ optional

1 Put the tea, mint and sugar in a teapot or jug and then pour on the boiling water. Leave to draw for a few minutes, remove the teabags, and then serve through a sieve. You can put in some mint leaves as desired.

2 For cool mint tea, add more water to the hot tea mixture and then place in the fridge. When serving, place a couple of ice cubes into each glass and top with mint leaves.

Serve with:

Chilied sweet potato and tomatoes p38
Savory banana snacks p138

Jamaica's *The Gleaner* newspaper reported that 'the Jones Town community has plans to turn dusty unoccupied land into oases of food and plants in keeping with the idea of eating what you grow.' This is something that is occurring in many parts of the world, and gives hope for feeding the growing population.

Ginger beer may conjure up Enid Blyton's *Famous Five* books for some of us, but perhaps that's why I'm so fond of it!

MAKES
4 cups/ 1 liter

TAKES
30 minutes + cooling time

Pack-a-punch ginger beer

V

1 large ginger root

4 sticks or 2 teaspoons cinnamon

4-6 cloves

1 cup / 240 g sugar

2 limes or lemons (juice and zest/peel)

4 cups / 1 liter water

1 Grate the ginger into a saucepan with the cinnamon, cloves, sugar, juice and zest of the limes or lemons. Then add the water.

2 Bring the pan to the boil, stirring from time to time. Now reduce the heat and simmer for 10 minutes and then allow it to cool.

3 Strain the liquid into a jug. Check the flavors, adding more water, lime or lemon juice, or sugar as desired.

4 Chill the drink and serve with ice cubes and slices of lime or lemon on top.

This cocktail is especially good for cooks! Its name refers to **Guyana**'s swizzle-stick, a small hand-whisk. Use a blender if you don't have one.

MAKES
2 glasses

TAKES
5 minutes

Rum swizzle with mint and lime

v

1 tablespoon superfine/caster sugar
2-4 tablespoons lime juice
2 sprigs mint
½ teaspoon cinnamon
3 tablespoons rum

Put everything, except one of the sprigs of mint, into a jug and swizzle away until the mixture is frothy (or use a blender). Pour onto cracked ice and decorate with remaining mint.

Goes well with... everything!

There's a website that helps you get non-meat meals in China. You can say *wo chi su* (literally 'I eat vegetables') and show the characters in case your intonation is faulty – here they are!

我吃素
WO CHI SU

If you are just traveling through Chinese food instead, you can pick and choose at the many Chinese supermarkets. When I visit one, the colorful wrappings and lettering are part of the draw! There are many intriguing snacks, like this crunch.

**MAKES
24-30
pieces**

**TAKES
20 minutes**

Sesame and peanut crunch

v

2 cups / 250 g unsalted roasted peanuts, chopped coarsely

½ cup / 50 g sesame seeds

2 cups / 450 g sugar

⅓ cup / 80 ml white wine vinegar

4 teaspoons water

rice paper

1 Start by toasting the sesame seeds. To do this, place a frying pan on the cooker without any oil or fat. Heat it and then put the seeds in and shake them around as they brown. They are ready when they begin to pop about. Set aside.

2 Then mix the sugar, vinegar and water in a saucepan over a low heat, stirring until the sugar dissolves.

3 Now bring the mixture to the boil and let it cook without stirring until it is golden and reaches 295-300°F/146-149°C, which is 'hard-crack' temperature. If you have no candy thermometer, test for this by taking a teaspoon and dipping it into the mixture. Then allow the syrup to drop onto a saucer of cold water. It should harden and snap with a clean break if it is ready. If it does not, continue to boil and test it again.

4 Grease a shallow baking tray 11 x 7 in/28 x 18 cm, and place rice paper on the bottom.

5 Mix the peanuts and half the sesame seeds into the sugar sauce and stir well. Then pour the mixture into the tray and sprinkle the remaining sesame seeds over.

6 Allow the crunch to cool slightly and cut it into small pieces. Then leave in the baking tray to cool and harden completely.

Grenada has plenty of nutmeg and bananas. Here's a helpful tip about bananas from a gardening forum: 'I have used bananas to ripen tomatoes in a drawer. It works well – apparently the bananas release a gas when they ripen which accelerates the ripening of other fruit in the vicinity, and for this reason you should keep them out of the fruit bowl so that your other fruit does not overripen and spoil.' Grenada is a major producer of nutmeg, used here.

SERVES
4

TAKES
20 minutes

Spicy baked bananas

V

4 bananas, sliced
  lengthwise
3 tablespoons lime juice
1-2 teaspoons sugar
1 teaspoon ground allspice
½ teaspoon grated nutmeg
½ teaspoon cinnamon
4 tablespoons rum +

+ optional

Heat oven to 375°F/190°C/Gas 5

1 Begin by greasing a shallow oven-proof dish. Then place the bananas in it.

2 Sprinkle on the lime juice followed by the sugar and spices. Pour in 3 tablespoons of the rum if using.

3 Bake for 10-15 minutes, basting from time to time. When the dish is on the table heat the remaining rum by holding the tablespoon over a flame until it ignites. Pour it over the bananas and serve when the flames subside.

INDEX BY REGION AND COURSE

Page numbers in **bold** refer to the main illustrated recipe.
Additional illustrations are shown by *italic* page numbers.

INDEX OF INGREDIENTS AND MEAL TYPES

red pimiento and pine nuts
128

PINEAPPLE/PINEAPPLE
JUICE
pineapple and avocado
salad 116
rum punch 190

PLANTAIN
vegetables in coconut milk
168

POTATO
coriander carrots and
potatoes 46
curried potatoes 64
gingery mashed potato with
yogurt 78
lentil and potato dhal 130
nutmeg potatoes 108
peppery potatoes with
eggplant/aubergine 114
piquant fries/chips 118
potato and bell peppers
with cumin 120
potatoes with miso 122
spicy vegetables in coconut
milk 146
spinach and potato
casserole 150

PUMPKIN
bean and pumpkin stew 20

cashew nut and pumpkin
salad 30
coconut milk pumpkin 40
pumpkin or butternut
squash soup 126
pumpkin curry 124

RAISINS/SULTANAS
banana bread 182
chocolate rum cake 188
gingerbread 200
lettuce and raisin salad 94
spiced apple chutney 144

RAITA
lentil and potato dhal 130

RED CURRY PASTE
tomato soup with beancurd/
tofu 166

RICE
coconut rice 42
fennel, rice and spinach 74
fried rice with beancurd/
tofu 72

ROSEMARY
red pimiento and pine nuts
128

RUM
chocolate rum cake 188
gingerbread 200

granadilla/passion fruit
cocktail 204
melon and kiwi fruit
daiquiri 212
rum punch 190
rum swizzle with mint and
lime 218
spicy baked bananas 222

SALADS/SALAD DRESSINGS
cucumber and sesame seed
56
lettuce and raisin 94
marinated cabbage 96
minted tomato and
cucumber 102
olive 110
peppercorn and eggplant/
aubergine 50
pimiento dressing 68
pineapple and avocado 116
tabbouleh 156
tomato 164

SAUCES
BEAN
sautéed eggplants/
aubergines in chili-bean
sauce 136
SOY
fried rice with beancurd/
tofu 72
sautéed eggplants/
aubergines in chili-bean
sauce 136

TAMARIND PASTE

spicy vegetables in coconut milk 146

TOFU see BEANCURD

TOMATO

bell pepper with eggplants/ aubergines and tomatoes 24

black-eyed pea/bean soup 26

casserole with green lentils 32

chilied sweet potatoes and tomatoes 38

kidney bean casserole 90

minted tomato and cucumber salad 102

mushrooms and ginger 106

peppercorn and eggplant/ aubergine salad 50

tabbouleh 156

tajine 160

tomato salad 164

tomato soup with beancurd/ tofu 166

yogurt piqued with mustard seeds and tomatoes 176

zesty topping 178

TORTILLAS

chili bean fajitas 36

TREACLE, BLACK

gingerbread 200

TURMERIC

beans with turmeric and coconut milk 22

black-eyed pea/bean soup 26

VEGETABLES, MIXED

couscous with 48

curry with coconut 104

hotpot with 88

kidney bean casserole 90

samosas 134

spicy vegetables in coconut milk 146

stir-fry with ginger 170

VINEGAR, WHITE WINE

sesame and peanut crunch 220

WATER CHESTNUTS

stir-fried veg combo with beancurd/tofu 152

YOGURT

carrot and yogurt dip 52

eggplant/aubergine dip 162

gingery mashed potato with yogurt 78

lassi 210

raita 130

tahini and yogurt dip 158

vegetables in coconut milk 168

yogurt piqued with mustard seeds and tomatoes 176

ZUCCHINI/COURGETTE

stir-fried veg combo with beancurd/tofu 152

About the author

Troth Wells is an editor, food writer, and cookbook author. She joined the *New Internationalist* in 1972 and helped to launch the magazine and build up its subscriber base. Later she worked as Books Editor, commissioning the *No-Nonsense Guide* series, and producing several highly-praised photo books. *Small Planet, Small Plates: Earth-Friendly Vegetarian Recipes* is her latest cookbook. Earlier bestselling cookbooks include *Global Vegetarian Cooking, The Spices of Life* and *One World Vegetarian Cookbook*.